THE ORANGE LEADER HANDBOOK

A THINK ORANGE COMPANION

REGGIE JOINER

David C Cook

transforming lives together

THE ORANGE LEADER HANDBOOK
Published by David C. Cook
4050 Lee Vance View
Colorado Springs, CO 80918 U.S.A.

David C. Cook Distribution Canada
55 Woodslee Avenue, Paris, Ontario, Canada N3L 3E5

David C. Cook U.K., Kingsway Communications
Eastbourne, East Sussex BN23 6NT, England

David C. Cook and the graphic circle C logo
are registered trademarks of Cook Communications Ministries.

The Web site addresses recommended throughout this book are offered as a resource
to you. These Web sites are not intended in any way to be or imply an endorsement
on the part of David C. Cook, nor do we vouch for their content.

All Scripture quotations, unless otherwise noted, are taken from the *Holy Bible, New International
Version*®. NIV®. Copyright © 1973, 1978, 1984 by International Bible Society. Used by permission of
Zondervan. All rights reserved. The author has added italics to Scripture quotations for emphasis.

ISBN 978-1-4347-6435-5
eISBN 978-1-4347-0186-2

© 2010 Reggie Joiner
Published in association with the literary agency of
D. C. Jacobson & Associates LLC, an author management company
www.dcjacobson.com

Portions of this book were originally printed in 2009 in *Think Orange*,
published by David C. Cook. ISBN 978-4347-6483-6

The David C. Cook Team: Don Pape, Amy Kiechlin, and Jaci Schneider
The reThink Team: Cara Martens, Mike Jeffries, Beth Nelson, Karen Wilson

Printed in the United States of America
First Edition 2010

1 2 3 4 5 6 7 8 9 10

122209

THE
ORANGE
LEADER
HANDBOOK

This manual is dedicated to church staffs around the country who have hosted and partnered with Orange to influence the next generation.

It has been inspired by every leader in every church who believes that ministry with children, teenagers, and college students is the most important work on the planet.

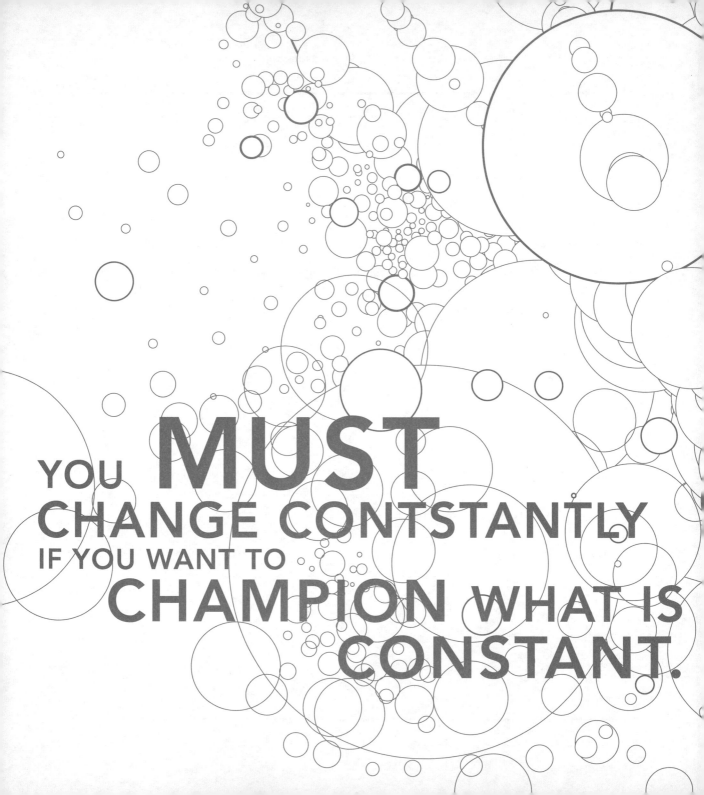

YOU **MUST** CHANGE CONTSTANTLY IF YOU WANT TO **CHAMPION** WHAT IS **CONSTANT.**

CHAPTER 1

Getting Started

CHAPTER 1

GETTING STARTED

WAIT.

READ THIS FIRST.

NO, REALLY READ IT.

DON'T READ THE REST UNTIL YOU READ THIS FIRST.

So many leaders have asked us, "What does an Orange church look like?"

On one level, it is any church trying to do a better job at partnering leaders and parents to influence the next generation.

On another level, many churches are taking the initiative to Orangify their strategies and are developing common characteristics.

This manual was written to identify those common characteristics and to help ministry teams establish a process to work on them consistently.

So ... what is an **Orange-ometer**?

It's a gauge, something you can use to
evaluate
tweak
adjust
and calibrate the important things you do.

Every ministry has systems that need to be updated frequently. What if you developed a habit of identifying and improving the systems that affect the most critical values of your organization?

You could significantly improve the way you

... work together as a team,
... communicate truth to children and teenagers,
... partner with parents,
... rally leaders to coach and mentor kids,
... affect the spiritual direction of a generation.

What if you started viewing certain systems as dials that have to be constantly fine-tuned in order to keep you moving in the right direction, controls that have to be frequently watched, touched, and adjusted?

It is important to recognize your potential to get stuck in an outdated, irrelevant style of ministry. It usually happens so slowly, you don't notice when you get comfortable, content, and satisfied with the way things are.

You start maintaining what was once created.

You start working from memory instead of operating from your imagination.

Think about how you would fly a plane:

Your hands steer. Your eyes watch the instruments. You constantly turn dials and move levers. Up, down, right, left. Some adjustments are incremental and others are more radical, but you do what you have to do to keep moving in the right direction.

Unless you want to get stuck in an outdated style of communication or programming, unless you want to get bogged down in an irrelevant ministry, you must be willing to do whatever you have to do to move in the right direction.

Change is inevitable:

the wind,
the environment,
the conditions.

The question is not "Will things change?" but "How will you adapt to change?"

As a leader, you need to morph, stretch, and grow. Accept that some things must evolve for the sake of what is timeless and unchanging.

Have you ever noticed that the nature of spiritual truth is often highlighted by what is temporary?

Have you ever considered the possibility that change makes the best platform to demonstrate what is eternal?

Change is not the enemy of what is sacred. Change is the *champion* of what is sacred.

Some people will get nervous and warn you, "Never change for change's sake." But if people don't see or

hear you anymore, maybe you should change whatever you need to change. If it gets their attention about what is true, if it makes them more aware of the mission, if it refuels their souls, it's worth it.

The truth is, you must never stop

re-examining,
re-imagining,
re-creating.

So don't use this Orange-ometer once; use it over and over again.

When you embrace the value of continual change in your culture, you open a door to radically improve your ministry. It may take time, but the work you do is critical and too important to not take seriously.

Remember, you are not just flying a plane; you are leading people spiritually.

So get serious.

Establish a team.
Identify the five core areas that should be monitored.
Use the thirty-five components to determine which area(s) need the most work.
Start turning dials as a team.
Keep fine-tuning and updating what you do.

Feel free to change labels or terms to suit your specific ministry. You can even rearrange the Orange-ometer itself to work better for your team. (We've given you some blank templates as well as completed ones.)

Just don't stop.

You must change constantly if you want to champion what is constant.

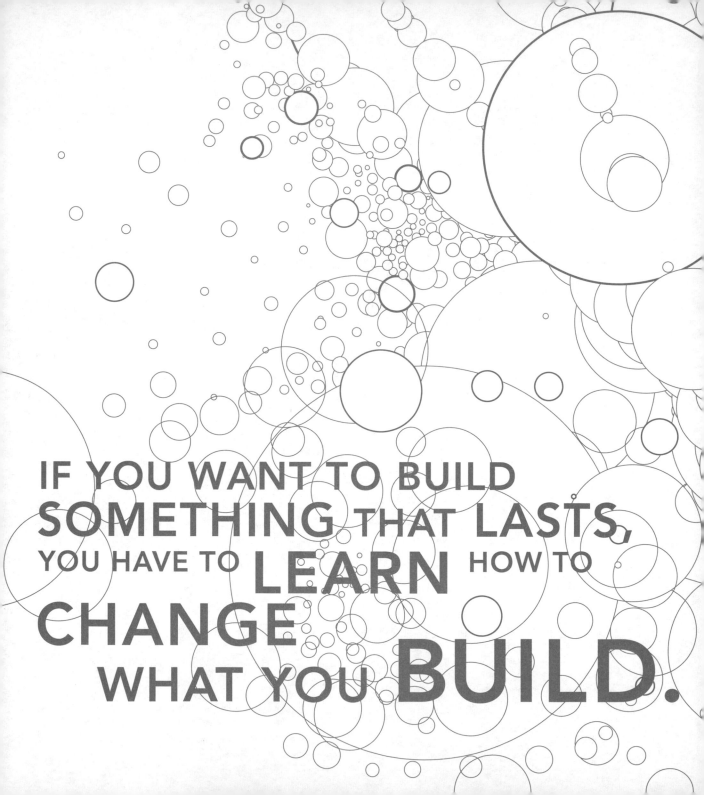

IF YOU WANT TO BUILD
SOMETHING THAT LASTS,
YOU HAVE TO LEARN HOW TO
CHANGE
WHAT YOU BUILD.

CHAPTER 2

Think Apples

CHAPTER 2

THINK APPLES

If you know anything about what we do, you know we talk a lot about the importance of "thinking Orange." Why Orange? Because we think there is a greater potential for impact if red and yellow are combined.

Here's what we mean: If the unconditional love of family (represented by red) works in sync with the light of the church (represented by yellow), we can be more effective in our influence with the next generation.

So why do we have a chapter about apples in a handbook about Orange? Contrary to popular thinking, it's smart to compare apples to oranges. For the sake of this chapter, when you think about apples, think about systems and change. You'll see why in a few paragraphs.

We all know that much of what worked yesterday in programming and ministry is not as effective today. This also suggests that what works today will need to change tomorrow. The question is, are we willing to create a culture of constant change within our ministries for the sake of connecting with people and culture?

Andy Grove was president and chief operating officer of Integrated Electronics Company (later Intel) in the late 1980s and early '90s. Integrated Electronics was one of the largest manufacturers of dynamic random access memory chips (DRAMs) in the world, but the computer industry was changing, and the company was losing business to Japanese manufacturers who made better, cheaper, faster chips. Rather than go down with the chip ship, Grove went to the chair of the board, Gordon Moore, and said something like this: The way we're going, we're all going to get fired because the company's going down fast. But let me ask you a question: What do you think the new guy coming into this organization is going to change? What do you think is the first thing he'll do when he walks in? Why don't *we* make those changes?

"The answer was clear," Grove said. "Get out of DRAMs. So I suggested to Gordon that we go through the revolving door, come back in, and just do it ourselves."[1]

And that's what they did. Over the next couple of years the bottom seemed to fall out of their organization. Their reorganization caused them to initially lose millions in profit, and they were forced to lay off thousands of employees. But after a few years the company began to recover, and the changes paid off as they became one of the fastest-growing companies in American history. What started that moment in Gordon Moore's office revolutionized Intel and saved the organization because they dared to say, "Let's walk out, walk back in, and make the changes that someone else will make after us."

It's a great question. If you could walk out the door of your ministry or church, then turn around and walk back in as the new leader, what would you change?

A senior pastor I know in Canada, Carey Nieuwhof, reminded me that the people who study the science of change think of it this way: People change when the pain associated with the status quo is greater than the pain associated with the change.

At some point, what it costs you *not* to change may outweigh what it would cost to change. At some point, you probably bought a cell phone because those gas station pay phones were disgusting, or you could never find enough quarters, or you didn't want to stop late at night. Or maybe you spent money on that expensive microwave because fixing dinner took you three hours, but it only took your neighbor thirty minutes.

I recently asked a group of fifty-year-olds about significant or interesting changes they had seen in their lifetimes. What changes have you seen in your lifetime?

NOTES

Their answers really focused the issue for me. Here are a few of them:
The Internet, Microwaves (that saved a lot of marriages!), Cell phones, Digital video recorders, Digital photos, GPS, iPhones, Facebook, The meaning of "green."

When you consider the amount of change in your lifetime, you're more adaptable than you thought you were. Just don't miss the point. In every scenario, you changed when the cost associated with not changing outweighed the price you had to pay to change. When it comes to our ministries, we tend to be slow to change because we underestimate what it will cost if we don't change. It is possible for us to embrace a style of ministry that becomes outdated simply because it is easier to maintain instead of change.

The truth is, **if you want to build something that lasts, you have to be willing to change what you build**. Admit it: You think everything you design is going to somehow stand as a lasting monument to your creativity. Sometimes the very thing we don't see as needing change is the *one* thing that needs to change so we can focus on what lasts forever. Your organization will be fundamentally different if you decide everything you've built should be open to change. That decision is magnified when you realize those changes are essential to strengthening what is important: the ideas and concepts that will remain after the programs and processes have been replaced.

I went up to the attic a while back and I found the Macintosh Plus I bought in 1986. It has a lot of sentimental value because I bought it right after we had our first child, our son. The Mac became a major resource for our ministry because at the time I was designing a lot of our materials for camp.

Before the Mac, I was doing graphics and layout on something called a Kroy machine. The Kroy had a big plastic wheel that would spin and print letters on a spool of tape. I'd make these long tapes of type and paste them onto paper. After I'd had more Kroy-filled all-nighters than I could count, Steve Jobs did an amazing thing: He invented the Macintosh computer.

I was a student pastor making less than $18,000 a year. (Maybe some things don't change!) My wife, Debbie,

THE ORANGE LEADER HANDBOOK

wasn't working since she'd just had our son. Her salary had been higher than mine, so we'd just gone down to less than half of our normal take-home pay.

Still, I knew we needed to buy that Macintosh Plus. Can you guess how much it cost in 1986? $2,600.

I guess we should have considered that a bargain. A man in our church owned a print shop and had just invested $100,000 in a new typesetting machine. The cost to lay out just one week of camp material using his typesetting equipment and personnel was going to be $1,300—half of what I'd pay for my Mac Plus. Within a year, his $100,000 machine was obsolete because of computers like mine. The desktop publishing movement transformed the five-hundred-year-old printing industry.

When I bought it, I didn't know anything about computers so I asked my dad to go with me. He was in the DOS-dominated world. (Mac users know that DOS stands for Dominion Of Satan). I remember when we went to the store, I asked my dad, "What size hard drive should I get?" I was trying to decide between twenty and thirty *megabytes*. He said, "Just get a twenty-megabyte machine … it's all you'll ever need."

If you were to come into my office right now and I was working on that old Mac Plus computer, you'd feel really sorry for me, wouldn't you? You'd feel for me what I feel for those of you still using Windows. The bottom line is that you'd think it was ridiculous, obsolete, that it no longer had any value. It's more than a quarter-century old. I want you who are younger to know this: This computer was an icon! It started a revolution. This was a powerful machine. It was a catalyst for a movement and now it's practically useless.

The good news is that the people who built the Mac Plus knew it was not the end goal. The Apple engineers never intended that early computer to last forever. It was designed to be temporary and created for a specific moment in time. They designed the Mac Plus with the mindset that it could connect with the state of culture right at that moment.

Some of those engineers may have suspected that Al Gore would one day create the Internet. Some may have projected that the postal system would change because of the digital age. Ultimately, this machine was built *not* to last because everything would change about the way we communicate. The day would come when the world could no longer be supported by something built in 1986.

The engineers, directors, and technicians who were involved in this process had a mission. Their mission wasn't to build a computer. It was more basic than that: It was simply to connect people to information they want and need every day. They had a mindset that things frequently and consistently need to change. Because that system would no longer support where things needed to go, they were going to have to create something else. The point is, they built it planning to change it.

Consider the MacBook Air. Have you seen it? Have you held one? It's an amazing machine, the first laptop with virtually no moving parts. It's also one of the thinnest computers available, able to fit into a manila envelope. In two decades, Apple went from the Mac Plus to the MacBook Air. How is it that a team of creative, smart people who put their time and energy and affection and heart and passion into the Mac Plus could create a culture that would someday get them the MacBook Air?

This didn't happen overnight or even in a year. It was a long process. But it was possible because of their mindset. It happened because Apple realized that over time you must upgrade.

Do you know how many system upgrades Apple made between the Mac Plus and the MacBook Air models? Incrementally, they made about eighty minor upgrades and a total of ten major upgrades. Do you know how many computers Apple developed between these two models? Almost sixty different computers to get from that point to this point. They were upgrading or changing something about their system three or four times a year.

So many times, we don't understand the value of change. We think it's something to be avoided. We have a tendency in the church world to build what we build with the idea that it should last forever. What would happen if your team sat around and started asking the question, "How can we make sure that as we're building, we're building with the mindset that it *should* change?"

I'm not picking on your staff or your church, because I don't know you. But I walk into some churches and I can almost name the year they got culturally stuck. Based on the smell and the furniture, it was 1979 when time stopped. Or in another church, the music and the order of the worship service says it stalled in 1993. These churches are convinced that what worked for them then should keep working for them now.

Some churches make the fatal mistake of thinking things should last longer than they really can. But what they really need is to make some changes. They need to upgrade their systems.

If you took a walk around your building or brought in some fresh observers for a Sunday service, is there anything in your environment or style of worship that shows you've gotten stuck in a previous time and haven't moved on?

NOTES

The best way to keep a team moving toward the central mission is to frequently upgrade the system. The next time you reach in and change something, remember that you're actually reminding yourself and the others on your team to focus on what is most important. The reason you need to change or upgrade is so you're frequently starting over again with your mission. In other words, if you're really trying to create something that lasts, you've got to back away on a regular basis and change whatever you need to change. And with every incremental upgrade, **you will be reestablishing and highlighting the mission in a clearer way**.

Think about it this way: For thousands of years God has used structure to emphasize what is transcendent. The Old Testament was a system of codes and laws that God used as a stage to amplify His redemptiveness. But that system was for a specific time, in a specific place, for a specific people. Systems need to be fluid, adaptable, and flexible. Changing form does not mean changing function, but the shape of the church at any time should be what God needs at that moment in history to accomplish His mission. Jesus came to challenge the system of His day, not to suggest there should not be any kind of system, but to emphasize that every system needs overhauling from time to time for the sake of a bigger mission.

We have to be willing to step back and realize why this is so important in today's church. We need to look at our churches and programs and see them as wineskins. We need to make sure everyone knows the difference between what is temporary and what is timeless. What are we going to do to make sure that we continue to demonstrate what is transcendent to the world? If our wineskins are old and not able to contain new wine, then we need to change the wineskins.

I sometimes hear people say, "The churches that are changing and innovative are abandoning what is timeless and sacred." Maybe the churches that *aren't* changing and innovative are the ones abandoning what is timeless and sacred. Over time, your responsibility is to make sure you are changing the wineskins and doing whatever you have to do to spotlight what is true. If you don't upgrade along the way, a timeless core principle might be lost. An entire generation may not hear or understand truth because you weren't willing to pay the cost to make changes.

Every church has critical systems that need to be consistently upgraded.

When we started North Point Community Church in Atlanta, I realized we needed a different approach to children and student ministries. After working in various models, I was convinced the church needed to be more effective at involving parents. I also became aware that specific systems needed to be upgraded if we hoped to effectively partner with families. Here's a list of some of those systems.

1   **The system that integrates your leaders.** How are you organized? How often do you meet? Is there a sense that your leadership structure is causing you to pull at each other? Is there alignment, everyone moving toward the same goal because you've created a system or a culture to that end?

2   **The system that communicates truth.** What is your basis for teaching and communicating? Have you created irreducible minimums for your content? Have you decided on the core truths you want each age group to understand and experience? Do you reinvent the way you create and present your message? Do you teach in a way that connects and engages?

At reThink, we decided we would create curriculums that were perpetual. We knew as soon as we put anything into a printed curriculum, it would get old quickly. We wanted a system of content that would be delivered every month online, content that was written just a few months before. We believe a system like this helps us be as relevant as we possibly can.

If you were to go back and look at a curriculum created three or four years ago, it would be like sitting in a room with an old, out-of-date computer. We know that we're responsible for handling truth—which is timeless—in a way that's very important. So we decided to handle what's timeless in a way that's perpetually changing (see myfirstlook.com, 252basics.com, xp3students.com for samples of our curriculums). Why? Because what changes has the most potential to highlight what is core.

3   **The system that connects people.** How do you build community? When it comes to how people do life together, does your system need an upgrade? If you were to do a survey, would people say, "We're not connecting. We don't feel like part of this community, and we're not finding other people to do life with in the context of meaningful relationships." What does your system look like when it comes to community?

4   **The system that partners your church with families.** Something is broken when it comes to how we interact with families. Many churches have systems that encourage parents to drop off their kids so the church can "fix" them spiritually. If the church doesn't effectively connect with parents and families, we won't have the necessary impact with the next generation. We need parents to actually start participating with the church in this mission.

5 **The system that mobilizes every generation to be the church.** Do you really believe that spiritual growth has as much to do with serving as it does with Bible study? If you do, then how does your programming reflect that principle? Do you primarily define your success by how many attend your classes or presentations? What percentage of your teenagers actually plug in to do ministry? Do you consistently tell adults and leaders that they will not grow spiritually if they do not find a place to serve? At North Point, Andy Stanley often says something like, "If you've been here for a couple of years and you're not serving, then you're not growing and so you probably better leave."

These are the five systems we explore in more detail in the book *Think Orange*. It has been exciting over the past few years to engage with a host of senior pastors and those who work with children and students who are constantly discovering fresh Orange insights related to these areas. Just remember as you think Orange that you need to think apples, too. Write this down somewhere you can see it often:

If you want to build something that lasts, you have to be willing to change what you build.

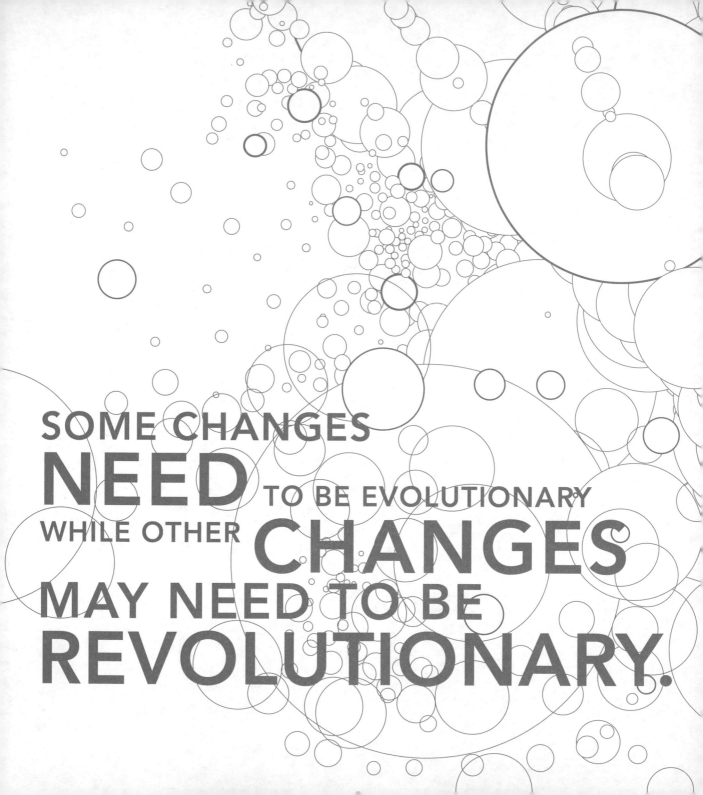

SOME CHANGES **NEED** TO BE EVOLUTIONARY WHILE OTHER **CHANGES** MAY NEED TO BE **REVOLUTIONARY.**

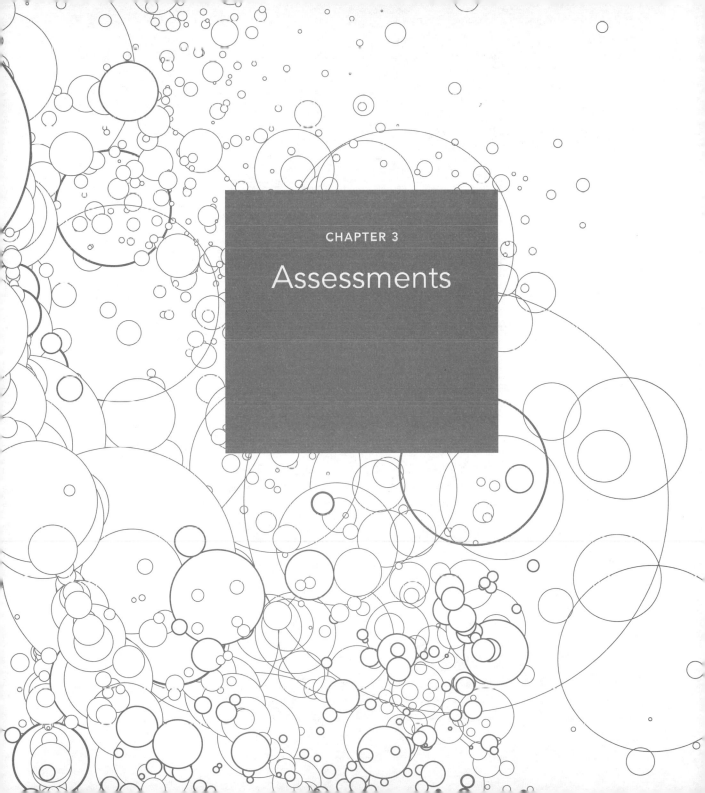

CHAPTER 3

Assessments

CHAPTER 3

ASSESSMENTS

Let's consider what it means to create a culture where your team practices the habit of upgrading. Remember at least these two things as you attempt to upgrade your systems. Once you have taken inventory of how your ministry is working, you usually make a choice to improve something or to add something:

1 **IMPROVE**
You upgrade when you improve the effectiveness or performance of something.

2 **ADD**
You upgrade when you raise something to a higher standard by adding or replacing a component.

In both scenarios your goal is to create a better version of what you currently have. In some cases your team will simply tweak something to work a little better, an incremental improvement in what you are already doing. In other scenarios, you may have to implement a new practice or add something that has never existed before. In that case you may find yourself taking time to design a new component to your ministry and also getting rid of the practice or element it will replace. Upgrading requires effective meetings in which your team not only dialogues but also establishes steps to implement the change. It all starts by creating an overall assessment of how key components work in your ministry.

Take a shot at evaluating the following thirty-five Component Statements and how well they describe your ministry. These are basic descriptions that provide a comprehensive overview of a typical ministry trying to shift to an Orange approach.

STRATEGY

ORANGE-OMETER

WHAT LEVEL OF EFFECTIVENESS DO YOU ESTIMATE YOU'RE REACHING IN EACH COMPONENT LISTED BELOW?

0 – Not happening
20 – Just getting started
40 – Making some progress
60 – Steadily moving
80 – In high gear

___**S1.** Key leaders from different age groups work as a team to manage an overall plan that connects various age groups.

___**S2.** It is clear who facilitates and leads the team that evaluates the effectiveness of ministries and programs for different age groups and families.

___**S3.** Meetings are scheduled on a consistent basis and are effective at keeping key leaders on the same page.

___**S4.** Specific phrases and terminology have been established so leaders, parents, and volunteers can articulate the philosophy and plan.

___**S5.** A short, concise phrase has been established for each age group, ministry program, and event so everyone is clear about its goal.

___**S6.** There is emphasis to stay simple and only do the few things that are strategic in leading people to groups.

___**S7.** A training plan has been established to continue to align leaders and parents and equip them around a common vision and strategy.

MESSAGE

ORANGE-OMETER

WHAT LEVEL OF EFFECTIVENESS DO YOU ESTIMATE YOU'RE REACHING IN EACH COMPONENT LISTED BELOW?

0 – Not happening
20 – Just getting started
40 – Making some progress
60 – Steadily moving
80 – In high gear

___M1. The curriculum emphasizes key spiritual concepts at the most age-appropriate time for children or students to learn them.

___M2. Age-group environments are designed to teach one key truth or single idea each week, which is amplified in a variety of creative ways.

___M3. The content taught is arranged and packaged so that presenters, large group leaders, and parents can talk about the same thing every week.

___M4. Emphasis is given to prepare and present content so listeners are able to connect timeless truths to their current experiences.

___M5. Those who communicate are consistently evaluated and coached so their messages are focused, personal, creative, and relevant.

___M6. Curriculums or content are evaluated on the basis of how effectively they can be implemented and discussed in the context of relationships with a consistent group of peers and a mentor or leader.

___M7. Physical environments have been designed to target the tastes of specific age groups and amplify key elements of the teaching and content.

MESSAGE

FAMILY

ORANGE-OMETER

WHAT LEVEL OF EFFECTIVENESS DO YOU ESTIMATE YOU'RE REACHING IN EACH COMPONENT LISTED BELOW?

0 – Not happening
20 – Just getting started
40 – Making some progress
60 – Steadily moving
80 – In high gear

___F1. The church positively communicates its expectations that parents are primarily responsible for their children's spiritual growth.

___F2. A pro-family culture is intentionally created through communication, the modeling of priorities, and the simplification of programming.

___F3. Resources, training materials, and small groups are leveraged to support parent issues and create continued learning opportunities.

___F4. There are consistent opportunities for families—parents and children/teenagers—to learn together in a shared experience.

___F5. Celebrations are strategically planned for parents and children to mark critical defining moments in their spiritual journeys.

___F6. Content and resources are leveraged as a catalyst for quality family time, so that core truths taught at church are also reemphasized at home.

___F7. Environments are appealing to unchurched families and have a positive reputation with the community outside the church.

COMMUNITY

ORANGE-OMETER

WHAT LEVEL OF EFFECTIVENESS DO YOU ESTIMATE YOU'RE REACHING IN EACH COMPONENT LISTED BELOW?

0 – Not happening
20 – Just getting started
40 – Making some progress
60 – Steadily moving
80 – In high gear

___C1. The entire church values the concept of building community through organizing kids and adults into smaller groups as a primary means of discipleship.

___C2. A core group of committed volunteers assume responsibility to invest in a child's or student's spiritual formation by leading a small group.

___C3. A high priority is placed on hosting consistent small groups for children and students to connect them relationally and spiritually with peers and a leader.

___C4. Small group leaders interact strategically with parents to establish a better partnership to influence the spiritual growth of children and students.

___C5. Leaders are encouraged to stay involved with the same group for multiple years, especially during middle and high school grades.

___C6. Small group leaders assume responsibility to model and lead students to develop personal habits related to prayer, Scripture, worship, and sharing their faith.

___C7. Students graduate with an awareness of their spiritual identity and a personal responsibility to own their own faith.

COMMUNITY

INFLUENCE

ORANGE-OMETER

WHAT LEVEL OF EFFECTIVENESS DO YOU ESTIMATE YOU'RE REACHING IN EACH COMPONENT LISTED BELOW?

0 – Not happening
20 – Just getting started
40 – Making some progress
60 – Steadily moving
80 – In high gear

___I1. Personal ministry and service are promoted and encouraged to volunteers as an integral part of the discipleship process.

I2. Leadership has created and managed a clear process through which students can plug in to consistent opportunities for ministry.

___I3. Adult volunteers effectively train and partner with children and students to help them serve—and even own—various ministry opportunities.

___I4. Annual series are specifically taught and designed to motivate and mobilize kids and teenagers to become actively involved in serving others.

___I5. Opportunities are highlighted for small groups and families to serve outside the church in the local and global community.

___I6. Leaders assume a responsibility to help students identify and use their gifts and talents in order to establish a personal mission mindset.

___I7. Children and students have an awareness of their roles in demonstrating God's story of redemption and restoration to a broken world.

FLYING WITH CHARLIE

A while back I got to fly with my friend Charlie Belcher on a King Air 350, a luxurious six-passenger turboprop plane. We were traveling from Daytona to Atlanta, and I was excited when he invited me up to the copilot's seat before takeoff. I have to admit being overwhelmed when I strapped myself in and looked around. Monitors, gauges, and lights covered every square inch of the cockpit. It was visual overload. I remember thinking out loud, "How did you ever learn how to do this?"

Charlie kind of laughed and began to tell me stories about his adventures as a pilot. Once we were up in the air, I motioned to the indicators again. "So how long does it take to learn how to do this?" What he said next made my heart skip.

"Oh, you can fly this right now if you want. I can usually tell pretty quick if someone has the talent to fly."

It sounded like a challenge. So before I could think about it, I grabbed the controls. Then my sanity kicked in, and I remember hearing myself back down.

"Are you sure I can do this?" I asked. Then I saw Charlie flip a switch and point to the monitor in front of me. It looked like the roof of a house on top of a triangle. The bottom half of the screen was green, and the top half was blue.

Charlie explained, "That's your attitude indicator. Keep the bottom triangle lined up with the angled lines. You pull your controls to go up. You push them to go down. Turn right to go right and left to go left. Oh, and don't forget … you want to keep the green half on the bottom and the blue half on top. If they switch places, that means you're flying upside down."

Charlie taught me some important lessons that day. As significant as each gauge was, the attitude indicator was primary. Nothing was more important than keeping my eye on the monitor in front of me and learning the basic essentials of going up, going down, and learning how to turn and control the speed of the plane. Until I learned those principles the rest of the gauges didn't really matter.

There are forty or more gauges in the cockpit of a King Air. Most of them are considered secondary indicators. Initially it was easy for me to get distracted and confused by the array of lights and panels. It seemed too complicated, when in reality flying is relatively simple. The average pilot solos after about twenty-five hours of flying with an instructor and gets a license after about fifteen hours of solo flying.

Sure, there are a number of checklists to learn, indicators to watch, rules to follow. But what it really comes down to is how well you can master the essentials.

UNDERSTANDING THE ORANGE-OMETER

On the following page we have provided an Orange-ometer graph. It is designed to give you a control panel for your ministry. At the top of each column is a word that represents one of our five Orange Essentials: Strategy, Message, Family, Community, and Influence. They are what we consider to be essential systems that need your constant monitoring and attention. They represent how …

You work together as a team (Strategy),

You communicate truth (Message),

You partner with parents (Family),

You build connections (Community),

You mobilize others to serve (Influence).

We are not suggesting these are the only systems that are important, but it's like flying an airplane: These are some primary functions you should master. They are essential if you want to influence the next generation and partner with the family.

Under each Orange Essential are seven components that are significant indicators of how well each essential is working. By transferring the Assessment scores on the previous pages to the Orange-ometer, you will provide your team with an overview of where you can improve your ministry.

Caution: Don't get so overwhelmed with the thirty-five components that you forget your primary focus. Until you understand the significance of the key essentials, the rest of the components really don't make any sense.

USING THE ORANGE-OMETER
By scoring your Orange-ometer, you can do some interesting things as a team.

Determine which of the five Orange Essentials you should give initial attention to. Averaging the score of your components at the bottom of each column will give you an indicator. We suggest you go to that section of the handbook and begin working with that essential first. (Note: If in doubt about where to begin, we suggest you start with the Strategy Essential and components.)

Circle the components that scored 0 or 20. They may indicate upgrades that need to be ADDED to your ministry. Consider setting aside some time to meet and discuss a plan of action to implement some of these as new features in your ministry. (For example, if you don't have a plan that provides teenagers "Repeated Opportunities" for serving, then consider meeting with a planning team to discuss how that could be implemented.)

Identify the components that need to be IMPROVED by using an asterisk. This indicates the components you can tweak and adjust to make quick improvements to your ministry. (For example, if you score low on "Strategic Teaching" or "Synchronized Content," you could look into subscribing to reThink's online curriculums for kids and teenagers, which can help you upgrade how and what you teach kids.)

Start with a short list of components (two or three) you want to give immediate attention.

You can download more Orange-ometer graphs from OrangeLeaders.com and even customize the terminology if you like, but the point is to have one overview that provides a quick look at what you are adjusting.

To help you focus on a few components at a time, we've created and included a planning sheet at the back of this handbook (download more copies at OrangeLeaders.com). On this sheet is a place to transfer the name of the component you're targeting and some questions to gauge the level from which you're starting. Apply this four-step process to help you come up with an action plan:

1 **INVESTIGATE**—Have an honest discussion with yourself and others about how you're really doing with this component.

2 **IDEALIZE**—Brainstorm ideas about how to improve this component or add it as a new feature if it's not yet part of your ministry.

3 **IDENTIFY**—Refine all your brainstormed ideas down to the best ideas.

4   **IMPLEMENT**—Establish an action plan with steps, assignments, and timelines.

DON'T GET DISTRACTED

Don't get preoccupied with all the components. Constantly review the essential issues and use the components strategically to improve those areas of your ministry.

Remember that small, incremental changes can really make a big difference.

Here are a couple of other important things to remember about the thirty-five components:

They are not denominational. They are not based on any kind of theological slant or perspective. The components are biblical in the sense that they are based on principles of leadership, the concepts of truth, and the need for relationships with others and family. But they are intended to be applications of core principles that are more practical than theological. They will translate to most church styles.

They are not based on church size. These are principles that are applied in start-up churches as well as megachurches. Nearly 70 percent of churches using these concepts have less than a few hundred people in total church attendance. Although some applications will look different in various size churches, those applying this strategy range from a few dozen in attendance to over twenty thousand. These Essentials are transferable, regardless of size.

THE NEXT STEP

So let's get started.

Take a few minutes and transfer your scores from the Component Statements to the Orange-ometer graph.

Match the prefix code at the beginning of each statement to the same code in front of each component on the graph. (For example if you score 40 on S1 on the Component Statements, put a 40 on the Orange-ometer graph next to "Synchronized Team.")

ORANGE-OMETER

In these spaces, transfer your scores from the Assessment pages earlier in this chapter. Calculate your average score and write it in the gauge at the bottom of each column. Begin working on the Essential in which your score is lowest.

GAUGE KEY

0 Not happening   20 Just getting started   40 Making some progress

60 Steadily moving   80 In high gear

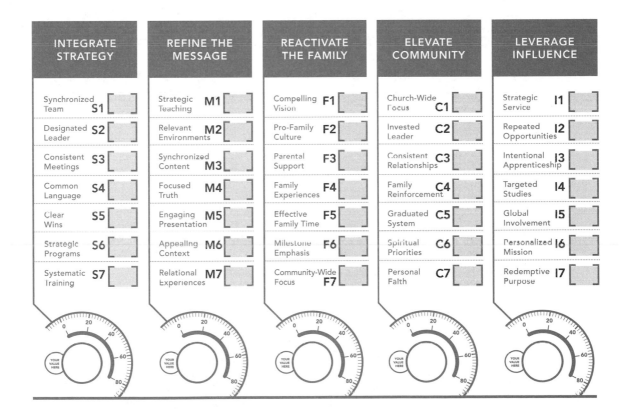

INTEGRATE STRATEGY	REFINE THE MESSAGE	REACTIVATE THE FAMILY	ELEVATE COMMUNITY	LEVERAGE INFLUENCE
Synchronized Team **S1**	Strategic Teaching **M1**	Compelling Vision **F1**	Church-Wide Focus **C1**	Strategic Service **I1**
Designated Leader **S2**	Relevant Environments **M2**	Pro-Family Culture **F2**	Invested Leader **C2**	Repeated Opportunities **I2**
Consistent Meetings **S3**	Synchronized Content **M3**	Parental Support **F3**	Consistent Relationships **C3**	Intentional Apprenticeship **I3**
Common Language **S4**	Focused Truth **M4**	Family Experiences **F4**	Family Reinforcement **C4**	Targeted Studies **I4**
Clear Wins **S5**	Engaging Presentation **M5**	Effective Family Time **F5**	Graduated System **C5**	Global Involvement **I5**
Strategic Programs **S6**	Appealing Context **M6**	Milestone Emphasis **F6**	Spiritual Priorities **C6**	Personalized Mission **I6**
Systematic Training **S7**	Relational Experiences **M7**	Community-Wide Focus **F7**	Personal Faith **C7**	Redemptive Purpose **I7**

TWO
COMBINED
INFLUENCES CREATE
SYNERGY.

CHAPTER 4

Integrate
Strategy

Align leaders and parents to lead with the
same end in mind

CHAPTER 4

INTEGRATE STRATEGY

ALIGN LEADERS AND PARENTS TO LEAD WITH THE SAME END IN MIND
Two combined influences create synergy

WHEN WE DON'T INTEGRATE STRATEGY

Parents struggle with how to partner with the church.

Programming and ministry tend to be random and isolated in impact.

There is no consistent forum to evaluate and change ineffective programming.

Leaders and volunteers get disillusioned with the lack of direction.

Staff members drift toward silo thinking.

Overprogramming and competing systems dilute the effectiveness of the church.

WHAT ELSE HAPPENS WHEN WE DON'T INTEGRATE STRATEGY?

I remember distinctly the day I became convinced that our church should become more intentional about partnering with parents. We were brainstorming ideas and in a moment of revelation, I realized that a lot of our leaders were not in sync. I thought, "We can't really expect parents to get on the same page with the church until we get on the same page as leaders." When ministries are divided by age, characterized by competing systems and disconnected staffs, there will always be limited success.

A strategy is a plan of action with an end in mind. That means you have identified what you want something (or someone) to be, and you have used your creativity and intellect to devise a way to get there.

Get your juices flowing … List some smart leaders and organizations. What are their missions, or what do they want to accomplish? What's their strategy? How do they get others to participate in the mission?

NOTES

In the *Think Orange* chapter on integrating strategy, we talked a lot about Nehemiah. I don't want us to forget that Nehemiah was not just on a mission—he had a strategy. So when you think in terms of *your* mission to influence the next generation, always remember …

It's the effectiveness of your strategy, not the scope of your mission, that ultimately determines your success.

What is your church and/or ministry's mission statement? Do you know it, or did you have to cheat and look it up? If you walked up to a new staff member or volunteer, would he or she be familiar with it? If your mission statement is what you're going to do, then a strategy statement is how you're going to do it. What are some "how" elements you can detail to describe the strategy you're pursuing?

NOTES

TRAFFIC CONES
Where are you leading people?

We are talking about those things used in your parking lot to help direct traffic and show people where to go. A lot of research has been done to determine why the cones should be painted orange. It's really amazing how a few pounds of orange plastic can control the direction of a two-ton car. The strategic placement of these orange cones guides hundreds of automobiles every day. If you really think about it, it's kind of like your leadership. You have been put in a position to lead others in a specific direction. So it's probably a good idea to spend some time figuring out where you want to lead them.

Nothing can wreak havoc like multiple parking cones scattered across the pavement in no particular order. The same idea applies to leaders who attempt to take people in different directions with no clear plan of action. It simply makes sense to work together. It is crucial to prompt frequent communication among all those who are in charge. Is your church characterized by competing systems and multiple staff members working in separate silos? Then start thinking Orange. Fluorescent, bold, traffic-cone orange to be exact! Start driving your meetings so your staff members are going in the same direction—that is, if you want them to lead people in the same direction.

A few misplaced traffic cones can confuse a lot of people and cause some nasty wrecks. Coming up with a good strategy is worth your time. Remember:

1 Traffic cones exist primarily to show people where they should go.

2 Traffic cones were designed to work together to have greater influence.

Get Real ... Take a stack of cones and talk honestly about your church and/or ministry from your visitors' perspectives. Do they clearly know the direction you're leading their families and what you want them to become? Where are you sending mixed messages about what you want them to do next? As a team, try labeling the cones with the key steps or programs you have in place so you have a visual.

NOTES

For a long time, I did ministry the way I first drove a motorcycle. I had a tendency to get so focused on what was right in front of me that I didn't see where things were ultimately leading and how everything should be connected. One of the most critical discussions you can have as a team is to decide where you really want to lead people. Where do you want them to end up? Back up and look at everything else in light of that one focus. What if all your ministries and all your families agreed about the focus? Wouldn't that change what you do and don't do?

NOTES

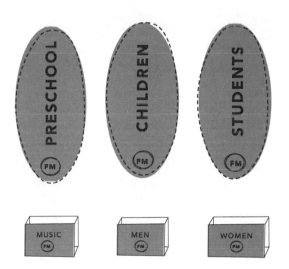

Departmental Model

In *Think Orange*, you can read in detail about different models found in churches (also in Concentrate 6.2 in *Think Orange*).

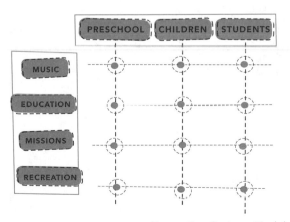

Competing Systems Model

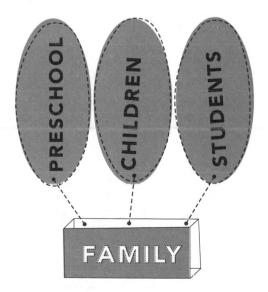

Supplemental Model

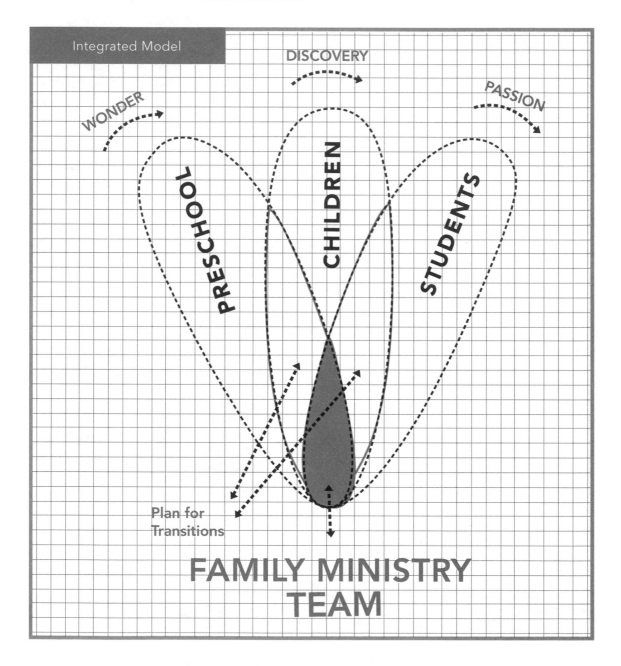

Integrated Model

DISCOVERY

PASSION

WONDER

PRESCHOOL

CHILDREN

STUDENTS

Plan for
Transitions

FAMILY MINISTRY
TEAM

In one of the first churches where I served, there existed a *competing systems model* (*Think Orange*, page 123). This setup created a complicated horizontal and vertical grid of positions and people—the result of a lot of written and unwritten policies.

Other churches have less overlap but are still too complex. In the *departmental model* (page 125), each department is independently responsible for creating programming and supporting families. The problem is that these efforts are random and the calendar crowded, which exhausts staff, volunteers, and the families they are trying to help.

Some churches have even formed a family ministry department separate from preschool, children, students, and adults. We call that a *supplemental model* (page 129), and it seems unnecessarily complex.

More than a decade ago, when we created North Point Community Church, we all recognized the need for a simpler system. We created a different model with three age-group ovals that overlapped at the bottom. This *integrated model* (page 127) requires collective intentionality to break out of a silo style of ministry. We'd consistently get together around a table, wearing our general, good-for-the-whole-church or ministry hats, not just our age-specific-specialist hats, to talk about things that affected all of us.

Important: Remember that your team doesn't have to be paid staff; it wasn't at North Point in the beginning. But when you integrate strategy, it expands everyone's capacity—including staff, volunteer leaders, and parents.

But a family ministry leader, someone like Nehemiah, needs to own the vision and live the strategy. This person will monitor the process—which may or may not involve managing the people—so all the players can live together on the same page.

After looking at these different models, draw what you think best describes your church's model at this point in time. Maybe looking at these models will help get you started. What are the advantages or disadvantages of your model? What about your model would you most like to change? What parts of it would you want to keep the same? Compare your drawing with drawings made by others involved in your church. Discuss the similarities, differences, and spoken and unspoken rules of your model(s).

DRAW

INTEGRATE

When we use the phrase "integrate strategy," we are suggesting that your plan of action should synchronize with the plans of others who are also in leadership. It implies you are combining multiple influences, primarily those in the home and church, and working off the same page for the sake of what you want to accomplish in the hearts of the next generation.

In *Think Orange* (page 132), there is a great visual of synergy at work. It's the power of two Belgian plow horses that are intentionally trained together versus the limitations of one or two untrained horses trying to pull all the weight on their own.

Think back to a time in your life or ministry when you've experienced this kind of synergy. What is one area in your ministry right now where you feel stuck, weighed down, and alone? Who could come alongside you and get on the same page so that you could move mountains?

NOTES

A few years ago, a friend who had been working to implement Orange thinking in his church called me late one night. He asked a simple question: "I think I understand the five Orange Essentials, but can you tell me what it would look like in my church?" He went on: "I just need to know what tangible components would be present in my church if we were implementing Orange thinking."

It took me a couple of long nights to get what he needed. The result was a simple list of seven components for each of the five Essentials that help clarify what it can look like when a church is becoming Orange.

I am not claiming that these are the only components, but they are some of the key ones. You can add your own. Change the wording or rearrange them if you like. The important thing is to establish a list as a point of reference to evaluate how you are doing and to know that each of these components will be in constant development.

I served at North Point Community Church for ten years. Do you want to know the truth about that church? Want to know the glue, the key, the secret? God did some amazing things that no book could ever explain, but I can point to one practical thing we did that really made a difference: The six of us who started the church met every Monday for two or three hours. And we didn't even like meetings. Sometimes, we didn't even like each other a lot. But we met every Monday for two or three hours. Why? The bottom line is we could not get on the same page if we didn't get in the same room on a consistent basis. And it's not just meeting, it's the kind of meetings you do—the kind where you are learning and pushing each other.

When I look back over a decade of meetings, one of the greatest things about them is not the fact that we agreed about everything, but that we agreed about the most important things. We agreed about the mission and values. We could debate changes and cultural things and it didn't cost us relationally. Why? Because we were all on the same page with the core issues. People on the outside of our church were a priority to us, to all of us. How we communicated truth and how we presented information in a relevant way was a priority for all of us. And because we had some big rocks in place that we all agreed about, those meetings were very powerful in keeping us aligned.

STRATEGY

THE SEVEN COMPONENTS WHEN YOU INTEGRATE STRATEGY
ALIGN LEADERS AND PARENTS TO LEAD WITH THE SAME END IN MIND

Getting everyone going in the same direction, toward the same goal, means committing to a strategy designed to deliver the destination. This involves the people you work with, how you work together, how often you work together, and what you talk about along the way. An integrated strategy is the starting point for the Orange way of thinking.

These seven components will help clarify what it can look like when a church is becoming Orange. Use them as points of reference to gauge how well you are doing in each area.

S1. SYNCHRONIZED TEAM

S2. DESIGNATED LEADER

S3. CONSISTENT MEETINGS

S4. COMMON LANGUAGE

S5. CLEAR WINS

S6. STRATEGIC PROGRAMS

S7. SYSTEMATIC TRAINING

SYNCHRONIZED TEAM

Department leaders and staff integrate as one team to establish and manage an overall strategy, as well as oversee age-group and family programming, calendars, and budgets.

I ask people all the time, Do you have a team? Who are the people responsible for making the decisions about the master plan, the strategy, and the end in mind? In your church or organization, where is the core team? It could be your senior pastor and a couple of staff members or it could include volunteer members. This team needs to incorporate leaders from each age group so a comprehensive plan is possible. It doesn't mean you don't have specialists for children or specialists for teenagers, but it *does* mean they're meeting together on a regular basis. If they aren't included and they aren't meeting, something's going to break down.

Who is on your family ministry team?

Who needs to be represented?

GAUGE KEY

0	Not happening
20	Just getting started
40	Making some progress
60	Steadily moving
80	In high gear

Align leaders and parents to lead with the same end in mind

S2

DESIGNATED LEADER

A specific leader is designated to facilitate the family ministry team's role in guarding alignment and improving overall strategy.

Part of developing an integrated strategy is having someone to integrate what could become divergent elements. This requires a single voice facilitating the plan, owning the importance of working together, and building vision for a single approach. Who owns the complete plan? Who is making sure that the preschool ministry, the children's ministry, the student ministry, and other ministries are working together and in sync with the master plan? This can be a senior staff member, a designated person on rotation, or even a key volunteer among other volunteers in smaller settings. Ultimately, though, you have to be able to answer the question, "Who owns this?"

Who is the designated family ministry team leader?

If you don't have a designated leader, who is on the list of possible candidates?

What specific criteria should your designated leader meet?

GAUGE KEY

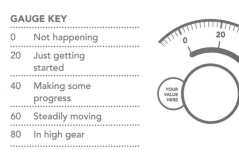

0	Not happening
20	Just getting started
40	Making some progress
60	Steadily moving
80	In high gear

Integrate Strategy

CONSISTENT MEETINGS

Meetings and/or off-sites are scheduled for consistent opportunities to work through a variety of critical issues the family ministry team should manage.

Not only do you need to have a team and someone to own the strategy and process of the team, you've got to meet. In person. On purpose.

The reason these meetings are important is because alignment doesn't just happen. *Misalignment* just happens; alignment requires intentionality. You drive your automobile a few thousand miles and you have to take it into the shop and get the tires realigned. Tires automatically start pulling against each other. The same is true in relationships. When you don't spend time with your kids, over time you drift apart. When you don't spend time with your spouse, working intentionally on doing things together, over time you pull apart. The same is true for any team in any church. If you don't spend time together in the same room, talking and wrestling with some of those issues, you'll start going off in different directions.

When are you meeting?

Are you meeting weekly or every other week using a consistent agenda to make sure you are talking about important topics?

Are you meeting monthly to review and focus on just one category?

Are you meeting quarterly for an off-site day and annually for a retreat to dream and think about the big picture? (This is time spent working on it rather than in it, which is what you do in other meetings.)

GAUGE KEY

0	Not happening
20	Just getting started
40	Making some progress
60	Steadily moving
80	In high gear

Align leaders and parents to lead with the same end in mind

S4

COMMON LANGUAGE

A common language is established to align leaders, parents, and volunteers to an overall mission and plan.

Along the way, we have to put together a set of terms so every volunteer and every parent can listen to our language and immediately know what we're talking about. For example, we have a phrase, "Teach less for more." It's a very specific principle about how we teach and why we teach what we teach. And if someone comes along and says, "I think we should do this, and talk about this," we can simply ask, "Does that fit with our 'teach less for more' principle?" Immediately, that brings everybody back, and they understand what we're talking about. If we say "small group" to a parent of a child or a high schooler, they know exactly what we're talking about because parents are in small groups. Investing in a common language will help you articulate your strategy in a way that everyone understands and will pay remarkable dividends in clarity and communication.

What phrases or terms identify your culture and philosophy?

What are the terms you've coined and use often that everyone understands?

Do you have a volunteer "glossary" with phrases and terms volunteers need to know?

GAUGE KEY

0	Not happening
20	Just getting started
40	Making some progress
60	Steadily moving
80	In high gear

Integrate Strategy

CLEAR WINS

A clear win is crafted for each age group, area, event, and program.

S5

What is the goal? What is the win? How do you know when you've reached success? When we're planning for a session, we take a creative board and say, "What's the win for this program for this environment? Let's all understand what the win is so we can plan everything in that light." How does that win move people relationally and spiritually to the end in mind? Ultimately, that's what a strategy is, and that's why a team has to sit around and wrestle with this.

A small group leader knows a clear win means leading young people to a place where they trust the wonder and discovery and passion of God. The mom who cooks hamburgers for the student program knows the win isn't a well-done cheeseburger, but a place where teenagers can hang out, be comfortable, and figure out what it means to be in relationship with God and others. How do you know when it's working? You won't know, unless you decide in advance what a victory looks like.

In the book *Seven Practices of Effective Ministry*, we devoted an entire chapter to what it means to clarify the win.[1]

Do your staff, key leaders, and volunteers understand the clear win every time they show up to serve?

When and where do you cast vision for your age groups, events, and programs?

Do you keep everyone connected with goals and celebrating wins? How?

GAUGE KEY

0	Not happening
20	Just getting started
40	Making some progress
60	Steadily moving
80	In high gear

YOUR VALUE HERE

Align leaders and parents to lead with the same end in mind

S6 | STRATEGIC PROGRAMS

Programs are evaluated on the basis of how they function as a step toward specific spiritual and relational goals.

Somewhere along the line, we bought into the idea that the more programming we do, the more stuff we have, the busier we keep our kids and students and families, the more effective we'll be. Just the opposite is true. What we need to ask is, Are we doing the few things that are most effective at leading people to the clear win?

When you have strategic programs instead of scattered programs, all your energy, focus, and resources zero in on one thing. Often in churches, we have multiple things sitting around all over the place that end up canceling each other out. They confuse people because they don't understand what path they should take. Every program you create should be a step in the direction you want them to go. Your job as a leader is not to take your ministry toward complexity but toward simplicity. The more complex your organization, the more competing systems you're going to have, and the more confused people will be about what's really important.

Do you have random programs that require you to manufacture energy to run?

If you discontinue one program, will it help another program's excellence level and participation increase?

Are there programs that need to be slightly or significantly changed in order to make them more strategic?

What might you put on a stop-doing list, a list of activities to cut out of your programming that will allow you to be more effective with your strategy?

GAUGE KEY

0	Not happening
20	Just getting started
40	Making some progress
60	Steadily moving
80	In high gear

Integrate Strategy

SYSTEMATIC TRAINING

Leaders, parents, and volunteers are given consistent training and vision to understand the overall strategy and their specific roles within the strategy.

One of the key questions we ask those who are upgrading is this: What are your primary sources of information? What are you reading? What are you studying? What are you learning? We're all one week away from being irrelevant unless we continue to learn. Learning together is part of that process of aligning and becoming a team. That's how we become a force collectively better than we could be individually. Resources are available from reThink and other organizations to help you and your team walk through the difficult questions and important action steps. Bring the team together. Talk about what's important. Learn from your leaders. Keep them pointed toward what really matters. These are essential aspects of training.

How often do you meet with leaders and parents?

What body of content do you want them to understand?

What is your plan for training new leaders?

How do you communicate vision to families the first time they visit your church?

What kind of apprenticeship structure do you have in place?

What kind of feedback loop do you have in place for leaders and parents?

GAUGE KEY

0	Not happening
20	Just getting started
40	Making some progress
60	Steadily moving
80	In high gear

Align leaders and parents to lead with the same end in mind

ACTIVITIES

THERE'S A GREAT SCENE IN THE MOVIE *FIRST KNIGHT* WITH SEAN CONNERY AND RICHARD GERE.[2] NOTICE HOW THE KING WAS CONSIDERED REVOLUTIONARY BY HAVING STRATEGY MEETINGS WITH HIS KNIGHTS AT A ROUND TABLE— WITHOUT HIMSELF AT THE OBVIOUS HEAD OF THE TABLE. WHAT CAN YOU LEARN FROM THIS PHILOSOPHY, AND HOW CAN IT SPILL OVER INTO YOUR FAMILY MINISTRY MEETINGS? (Here's a sneak peek below.)

KING ARTHUR: Here we believe that every life is precious, even the lives of strangers. If you must die, die serving something greater than yourself. Better still, live ... and serve.

LANCELOT: The Round Table.

KING ARTHUR: Yes. This is where the High Council of Camelot meets. No head. No foot. Everyone equal ... even the King.

LANCELOT: (Reading the inscription on the table) "In serving each other, we become free."

KING ARTHUR: That is the very heart of Camelot. Not these stones, timbers, towers, palaces. Burn them all ... Camelot lives on. Because it lives in us. It's a belief we hold in our hearts.

YOU'RE INVITED!

Who needs to be on your family ministry team?

....

....

Who would contribute a lot to the conversation as a generalist and specialist?

....

....

When will you meet?

....

....

How regularly will you get together, and where?

....

....

P.S. Think outside the box to unpaid leaders and even people you regularly disagree with about scheduling or use of resources. Maybe this would help you work together more proactively.

IF YOU REALLY WANT TO SEE HOW INTENTIONAL AND STRATEGIC YOU'VE BEEN AS A CHURCH OR MINISTRY, LOOK FOR CLUES IN YOUR CALENDAR AND YOUR BUDGET. GRAB SOME HIGHLIGHTERS AND CALCULATORS AND SEE WHERE YOUR TIME AND MONEY ARE BEING SPENT.

To take it a step further, think about a first-time guest or someone outside your organization looking at this with you.

WHAT WOULD HE OR SHE THINK YOUR PRIORITIES WERE?

WOULD THE GUEST FEEL VALUED OR STRESSED BY THE RESOURCES BEING SPENT AND THE SCHEDULE THAT'S BEEN CREATED?

(As a project, consider having your staff members selectively walk alongside these outsiders in the process.)

ACTIVITY: CREATE A STOP-DOING LIST

What are some things you should stop doing so you can do some other things better?
The things you have to manufacture energy for to keep going should top the list.
Intuitively, you know these things are keeping something else from working. Be bold.

Write them down with a date when you want them to stop.

ORANGE-OMETER

In these spaces, transfer your scores from the component pages earlier in this chapter. Calculate your average score from the seven components and write it in the gauge below.

GAUGE KEY

0	Not happening
20	Just getting started
40	Making some progress
60	Steadily moving
80	In high gear

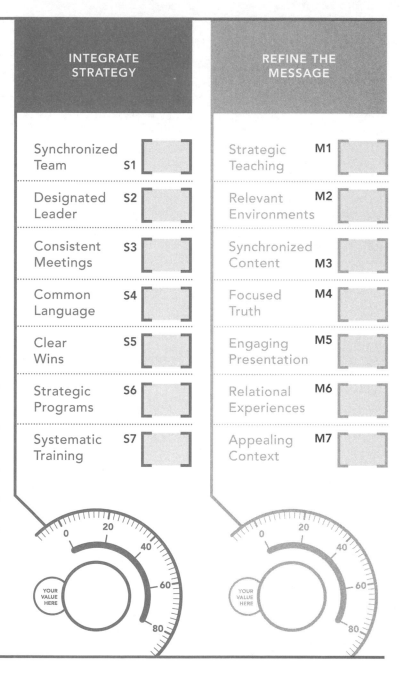

INTEGRATE STRATEGY

Synchronized Team	S1	
Designated Leader	S2	
Consistent Meetings	S3	
Common Language	S4	
Clear Wins	S5	
Strategic Programs	S6	
Systematic Training	S7	

REFINE THE MESSAGE

Strategic Teaching	M1	
Relevant Environments	M2	
Synchronized Content	M3	
Focused Truth	M4	
Engaging Presentation	M5	
Relational Experiences	M6	
Appealing Context	M7	

YOUR VALUE HERE

YOUR VALUE HERE

REACTIVATE THE FAMILY	ELEVATE COMMUNITY	LEVERAGE INFLUENCE
Compelling Vision **F1**	Church-Wide Focus **C1**	Strategic Service **I1**
Pro-Family Culture **F2**	Invested Leaders **C2**	Repeated Opportunities **I2**
Parental Support **F3**	Consistent Relationships **C3**	Intentional Apprenticeship **I3**
Family Experiences **F4**	Family Reinforcement **C4**	Targeted Studies **I4**
Milestone Emphasis **F5**	Graduated System **C5**	Global Involvement **I5**
Effective Family Time **F6**	Spiritual Priorities **C6**	Personalized Mission **I6**
Community-Wide Focus **F7**	Personal Faith **C7**	Redemptive Purpose **I7**

YOUR VALUE HERE — 0 20 40 60 80

YOUR VALUE HERE — 0 20 40 60 80

YOUR VALUE HERE — 0 20 40 60 80

TWO
COMBINED
INFLUENCES AMPLIFY
WHAT'S IMPORTANT.

CHAPTER 5

Refine the Message

Craft core truths into engaging, relevant, and memorable experiences

CHAPTER 5

REFINE THE MESSAGE

CRAFT CORE TRUTHS INTO ENGAGING, RELEVANT, AND MEMORABLE EXPERIENCES
Two combined influences amplify what's important

WHEN WE DON'T REFINE THE MESSAGE

Parents and leaders will probably never teach the same truths in a synchronized effort.

The church is perceived as irrelevant.

Individual leaders will tend to teach whatever they think is important.

A canceling effect happens to important core truths.

Biblical truths are viewed as boring and outdated.

Students pursue spiritual insights in other ways.

There is a failure to experience truth in a way that results in life-change.

WHAT ELSE HAPPENS WHEN WE DON'T REFINE THE MESSAGE?

CARROTS
How are you presenting the truth?

Funny thing about carrots—for centuries they were not a very popular food. That may have been because of their color. Up until the sixteenth century, carrots were grown in a variety of hues: red, black, yellow, purple, and even white. Then Dutch farmers married some yellow and red carrots to produce our modern-day orange carrots in honor of their king, William of Orange.

I imagine there must have been some orange-carrot skeptics in the beginning. They were probably overheard saying things like:

"These can't be true carrots."

"Carrots aren't supposed to look like that."

"Those are not the kind of carrots my parents ate."

Nevertheless, the color of carrots changed forever. But *changing the color of carrots did not alter the fundamental nature of the carrot.* In other words, orange carrots were just as nutritious as black carrots. The only real difference between the two was that more people were willing to eat orange carrots than black ones.

If you knew more kids and students would engage in what you teach if you packaged it differently, would you?

Would you color it Orange if more kids would listen?
Before you start using phrases like "watering down the truth" or "not deep enough," just remember that you can change the color of something without compromising its nature. It doesn't mean you weaken your message just because you focus on what your audience needs. The principle is clear. If you want more people to eat carrots, then change the color. If you want more students to listen to what is true, change how you present it.

It's okay to communicate in a way that's fun.

It's smart to use language they can understand.

It's responsible to believe that how you teach the truth may determine whether or not it's actually heard.

Get the juices flowing … Brainstorm a list of things that smart parents and/or marketers have "colored" to make something more appealing to their audience *without altering the content or product itself.*

NOTES

One of our favorite quotes about refining the message comes from Andy Stanley in his book *Communicating for a Change*:

"How you say what you say is as important as *what you say."* [1]

Take one of your favorite quotes and analyze it. What makes it so memorable? Think about the last sermon you heard or the point of the lesson you taught for children this week. Does any line or phrase stand out in your mind? If you stopped a child and asked about it, what would he or she remember?

NOTES

Words are powerful. We have the potential to say things in a way that will make a lasting impression, a bad impression, or in some cases no impression at all. If there are any two entities that should work hard to leverage words effectively, they are the church and the home. What we have to say is more important than anything.

We all have sound bytes that play in our heads from time to time, words that have stuck with us for good or for bad. Can you think of some words that have made a lasting impression on you? What have those words encouraged or discouraged you from doing?

NOTES

We need to be aggressive at reinventing what we say so that it will be heard and internalized—or students will suffer from a "white noise" effect in that they have heard a message for so long they just don't hear it anymore. If you want people to hear you, you may have to change your language before you change your presentation.

When or where does white noise have an effect on you, so you find yourself tuning out? What signs would you look for in the kids and students in your ministry to see if they were tuning out versus being actively engaged with the message? Check for levels of engagement this week during key times. Have a few different people observing this so you can discuss later.

NOTES

SYNCHRONIZE

It is important to refine your message to a few core components that help parents and leaders stay focused on the bigger picture. When you use the same terminology to show the foundation of your content from preschool to students, it amplifies the big picture of what you are trying to say. It helps everyone—staff, leaders, and parents—understand the value of a comprehensive plan.

When it comes to our message, we should teach with the same end in mind. What the church and the home have in common is the potential to create an environment in which children can be consistently reminded about God's story. How we say what we say, when we say it, and how we say it together amplifies our message like surround sound in a child's or student's heart.

LESS IS MORE

"The ability to simplify means to eliminate the unnecessary so that the necessary may speak."
—German expressionist painter Hans Hofmann[2]

There are about
800,000 words in the Bible.
600,585 words in the Old Testament.
180,552 in the New Testament.

But only 25,000 of Jesus' words were actually recorded. Those words changed the world then. They are still changing the world now. So you can say less and still make an impact.

Jesus boiled everything down to what is most important.

"Love the Lord your God with all your heart and with all your soul and with all your mind. This is the first and greatest commandment. And the second is like it:

"Love your neighbor as yourself."[3]

Think about these three different age groups: preschool, children, and students. Write down on Post-it notes some of the "big rocks" you want them to walk away with. What do you think they need to know? What do they need to understand, and what do they need to be able to do spiritually to impact their worlds? Move the Post-it notes around under the different age groups as you discuss or think about it.

NOTES

At reThink, we've created a comprehensive plan that keeps the end in mind and takes into account the different needs (or "big rocks") that need to be in each stage. The Great Commandment served as our model for the priorities in our strategy and helped us determine a win for those who teach or lead children.

WONDER
preschool
What would happen if your children grew up amazed with the wonder of their heavenly Father and how much He loves them? What if they understood God is big enough to handle whatever they will face in life? You want them to truly love God.
www.myfirstlook.com

DISCOVERY
elementary school
What would happen if your children felt challenged to pursue a lifestyle of discovery, in which their identity is determined by a personal relationship with Christ and they are guided by His Spirit? You want them to find their purpose in Christ.
www.252basics.com

PASSION
middle and high school
What would happen if your kids developed a sense of passion that mobilized them to do what Jesus did on Earth? What if they understood they are designed to personally participate in God's story to show His redemptive plan to every generation? You want them to love others the way God does.
www.xp3students.com

Whenever you read Jesus' sermons and hear His conversations, you get the sense that everything He said was said for a reason. He had a way of simplifying complicated truths so people could see God in a way they never had before. There were times He didn't explain what He meant, and He left them with the mystery. Other times He used powerful object lessons, and then He gave His words to twelve followers and told them to keep telling His story. Then His message became even louder.

Here's a list of five principles to keep in mind as we refine our message:

1

SAY LESS
WHAT ARE YOU GOING TO SAY?

Simplify what you need to communicate to the biggest concept.

Teach less for more. Take everything down to the "irreducible minimums." In our curriculum we call this the bottom line. Sometimes we think it's our job to teach the entire Bible. It's not. Some parts are more immediately relevant for a child or student than others. All Scripture is equally inspired by God, but all Scripture is not equally important.

If you could only teach one Bible story or principle, what would it be? Does it matter if the age of the audience changes? Check out how your curriculum is organized. Is there a comprehensive plan from cradle to college?

NOTES

2

SAY WHAT MATTERS
WHY ARE YOU GOING TO SAY IT?

Predetermine your content on the basis of relevance.

I haven't run into many non-Christians who don't go to church because it's too relevant. I hear descriptions like "boring," "old," "can't fit in," and "judgmental," but not the word "relevant." Instead of running into churches that are too relevant, I tend to see the fallout from people who claim the church is irrelevant.

Churches have a bad habit of sacrificing the potential that exists in timeless, life-changing truths because they fail to communicate those truths in a relevant or helpful way. We are notorious for answering questions people are not asking.

It's like …
giving a drink of water to someone who is cold …
handing jumper cables to a man with a flat tire …
telling a story to someone who is bleeding.

Whether we are church leaders, parents, or teachers (and whether we work with preschoolers, kids, or teenagers), we must all learn to ask this question: Is this really helpful or relevant to this person's season of life? Either you are trying to teach the Bible to children and students, or you are teaching children and students the

Bible. This may sound like the same thing, but it is really very different. In the former case, you start with the Bible and try to present it to them unfiltered. In the latter, you begin with the lives of the children and students and help them see how applicable the Scripture can be.

If you write your own curriculum (even occasionally), do you first pick the passage/principle that you want to teach and then try to make it apply to your target audience? Or do you start by deciding what they most need to know *right now* and then look for specific truths in Scripture that would apply to their lives and relationships?

NOTES

**3 SAY IT CLEARER
HOW ARE YOU GOING TO SAY IT?**
Craft words that capture the power of the principle.

We live in a media-driven generation in which people grab powerful words and hold onto them. Just check out people's Facebook pages and read their favorite quotes. You don't see a lot of fluffy or wordy sentences that go on forever. You see phrases from poems, punch lines from movies, statements from famous people, and something someone said on TV last night. The cultural world around us is reinventing how it says what it says all the time. Writers will go on strike over intellectual property and millions of dollars will be spent, all because of the power of words. We brand them, sing them, wear them, film them, drive them, graffiti them, buy them, sell them, claim them, and speak them.

So please, manage your words carefully and creatively. A lot is at stake.

Habits of Effective Teaching

Here are some specific ways we apply principles of refining the message in our curriculum so every leader and communicator can be a more effective teacher:

IMPRESS: Make it Big
What is the one thing you want them to understand? Make sure everything you do reinforces the main principle.

APPLY: Make it Fit
What do you want them to walk away and do? Show them how what you say fits into their everyday lives.

RECYCLE: Make it Stick
How will you make sure kids never forget? Once you have created the right statements, repeat them until they stick.

EXPERIENCE: Make it Theirs

How will you help them make the message their own? Sometimes it helps to not say it, but instead to create an experience that facilitates learning.

PERSONALIZE: Make it Real

What can you model for them from your own life? A personal example may illustrate a point more clearly than a thousand other words.

TRANSITION: Make it Flow

What will you say or do to keep them engaged? Shifting smoothly between different elements is vital to keeping kids' attention.

4 DON'T SAY IT
WHAT IS THE BEST WAY TO NOT SAY IT?

Create an experience so the message can be processed.

If we could explain everything there is to say about God, then He wouldn't be God. If that's true, then why does it bother us so much if we can't always be the teacher with all the answers? Rick Warren of Saddleback Church says, "Today, seekers are hungry for symbols and metaphors and experiences and stories that reveal the greatness of God. Because seekers are constantly changing, we must be sensitive to them like Jesus was; we must be willing to meet them on their own turf and speak to them in ways they understand."[4]

Have you ever experienced something powerful that had few, if any, spoken words? What was the impact on you? If you looked at what you're teaching this week, what part of your message could you play with so that you say very little, if anything, but still get your point across? Later, ask for feedback and ideas from children, students, or volunteers on this change.

NOTES

5 SAY IT LOUDER
WHERE ELSE CAN YOU SAY IT?

Leverage every possible environment to reinforce each concept.

An interesting relationship exists between content and environment. You can read more in *Think Orange* starting on page 147 about the process and thinking behind the children's space on the North Point campus, but the point was simply to give kids a visual cue that would create anticipation and make some primary truths stick in their hearts. Context can really have a way of highlighting the message and story of God.

Walk through your preschool, children's, and student environments. Go down each hall on your campus and into every room. Take some notes. What is being communicated loud and clear? If you're feeling really brave, walk with someone from outside your organization and get honest first impressions. Based on the space (the layout, the resources, the condition), how valued does the next generation seem to your church?

NOTES

Too many times we think only about a formal presentation like the main teacher or the more formal areas like the welcome center or large group stage. But that only represents one or two parts of what children in our care experience on Sunday or during the week's events.

What other roles or places can we emphasize in our environments to communicate our ministry values and weekly principles? Do the greeters as well as the large group leaders and large group communicators all know the same plan, this week's bottom line, and the Bible story?

NOTES

Put it to music, put it on the walls, put it in their hands, put it in the car, put it in their homes, and most importantly, give it to parents so they can talk about it in the context of a loving relationship at home. Truth is learned best in this circle of significant voices.

These statements are the foundation for all our curriculums. The truths are applicable to all age groups, but we emphasize specific ones at certain times in life. See *Think Orange* Concentrate 7.4 for more details on the Basic Truths.

PRESCHOOL

God made me.

God loves me.

Jesus wants to be my friend forever.

CHILDREN

I need to make the wise choice.

I can trust God no matter what.

I should treat others the way I want to be treated.

STUDENTS

I am created to pursue an authentic relationship with my Creator.

I belong to Jesus Christ and define who I am by what He says.

I exist every day to demonstrate God's love to a broken world.

WONDER
Discovery
Passion

Wonder
DISCOVERY
Passion

Wonder
Discovery
PASSION

MESSAGE

THE SEVEN COMPONENTS TO REFINE THE MESSAGE
CRAFT CORE TRUTHS INTO ENGAGING, RELEVANT, AND MEMORABLE EXPERIENCES

What are we communicating? How are we communicating it? Are we really spending the energy and the time that we need to craft a message the next generation hears? Many of you spend an extraordinary amount of time moving toward an event or an environment. A huge part of that is your content—what you're going to communicate and what you're going to teach. So it makes sense to back up and, if you're honest enough, make some decisions.

These seven Components will help clarify what it can look like when a church is becoming Orange. Use them as points of reference to gauge how well you are doing in each area.

M1. STRATEGIC TEACHING

M2. RELEVANT ENVIRONMENTS

M3. SYNCHRONIZED CONTENT

M4. FOCUSED TRUTH

M5. ENGAGING PRESENTATION

M6. RELATIONAL EXPERIENCES

M7. APPEALING CONTEXT

M1

STRATEGIC TEACHING

A curriculum plan is organized around the critical core concepts that are most important for an individual age group to understand and embrace before they leave.

When a college student is sitting in his freshman dorm room looking back across his experience at the church, what things will he remember? What things will you have taught him? In that moment, when he is getting ready to make a decision, what principle will he reach in and draw from? The reason we've determined the most important teaching elements for preschoolers, children, and teenagers is because we believe we should highlight core biblical truths that are critical for each age group.

If "integrate strategy" means we should lead with an end in mind, "refine the message" means we should teach with an end in mind.

Think about a clear win—what you want the end to be—and teach that way. When we developed our First Look, 252 Basics, and XP3 curriculums, we wanted a strategic plan that worked for every age group in a different way. We're not going to teach children the same thing we teach high schoolers. We think all kids need to understand some things before they are four or five years old, and children should embrace certain truths before they reach eleven or twelve. When they hit middle school and high school, they need to access another set of core information, but it all comes back to the big rocks—the priorities—Jesus put in place that day when He spoke the Great Commandment.

Do you have a ministry overview so everyone knows where you're going?

Are the reasons for the curriculum scope evident and understandable?

Do leaders, parents, and even students understand why you're not teaching the entire Bible to every student?

GAUGE KEY

0	Not happening
20	Just getting started
40	Making some progress
60	Steadily moving
80	In high gear

Craft core truths into engaging, relevant, and memorable experiences

M2 RELEVANT ENVIRONMENTS

Leaders, volunteers, and parents are trained to prioritize and articulate the overall teaching strategy and synchronize in teaching key truths.

Relevance has to do with how you connect truth so children, students, and families can see how it applies in their lives. We think teams should spend a lot of time around a table asking themselves this question: Is this environment or this weekly production helping move a student from here to here? You can't force anybody to have a relationship with God. You can't even force people to have relationships with each other. But what you can do is create an environment that makes those relationships more accessible.

The first chapter of John says some important things about why Jesus came to this planet. It says He was the true light that gives light to every man, that He was God, and that He came from the Father. Without getting into some heavy theology, I think it is safe to conclude that Jesus did two extraordinary things: He turned on a light spiritually and He built a bridge relationally. He helped people see what was true and He helped people know God. As leaders, we should attempt to do the same thing. What would happen if you left every environment and simply asked the question, Did we turn on a light to help people understand a key truth? Did we build a bridge to help them connect to God in a better way?

Do each of your age groups understand the overarching themes you keep coming back to?

Can your leaders communicate the "big three" for each age group?

What aspects of your environments point people to what's most important?

GAUGE KEY

0	Not happening
20	Just getting started
40	Making some progress
60	Steadily moving
80	In high gear

Refine the Message

SYNCHRONIZED CONTENT

Each age group has specific teaching content that is arranged and packaged so that communicators, large group leaders, and parents are able to talk about the same thing every week.

Something powerful happens when your large group leaders, your lead communicator, and your parents are all saying the same thing at the same time. What do you do in your organization to leverage what you teach on a weekly basis so parents can understand it and participate in it? It is powerful and significant for parents to understand what you teach and why you teach it.

Think in terms of how you can get more voices saying the same thing at the same time. Remember, if you only have forty hours in a given year to influence a life, you have to *synchronize* in order to make a greater impact. When those who present the truth make sure it connects with what large group leaders are discussing or illustrating, you are synchronizing. When parents talk at home about the same thing leaders teach at church, you are synchronizing.

How are you helping leaders and parents know the bottom line each week?

In what ways can you have more people saying the same thing at the same time?

GAUGE KEY

0	Not happening
20	Just getting started
40	Making some progress
60	Steadily moving
80	In high gear

YOUR VALUE HERE

Craft core truths into engaging, relevant, and memorable experiences

M4 FOCUSED TRUTH

Each weekly environment is designed to teach one key truth that is amplified through presentation and group discussion.

Instead of standing up in front of an audience and giving a list of seven things to do with a biblical passage, we like to narrow it down to one primary truth. Instead of saying, "This is the story of Joseph, and there's Joseph in the pit, and there's Joseph and Potiphar's wife," we zero in on reconciliation or forgiveness and why it's so important.

Sometimes when we teach with multipoint lists, we cause a canceling effect. Multiple points actually have a way of distracting from what is most important. So make sure you build everything around a clear bottom line or principle. (Andy Stanley explains this "one point" teaching concept in his book *Communicating for a Change*.)

We want people to walk away and remember one thing that changes their lives. We call it "teach less for more," but it's the idea of one truth at a time. Every week, there should be a *focused truth* everybody knows—the idea we want a teenager to grapple with, a child to remember, and a preschooler to learn.

How can you focus on a single principle instead of a multipoint list?

What percentage of time do you spend on information or application when teaching children or students?

If you are not the one communicating the message, how much advance time does the person who will be communicating have to work with the content?

Does the communicator use personal examples or share how this content translates in his or her everyday experience?

GAUGE KEY

0	Not happening
20	Just getting started
40	Making some progress
60	Steadily moving
80	In high gear

Refine the Message

ENGAGING PRESENTATION

Communicators are consistently coached and evaluated on the focus, authenticity, creativity, and relevance of their messages.

As you're refining your message, dare to ask yourself these questions: Did they pay attention? Did they listen? Did I engage them? How did I present it in such a way so they would stay with me?

Please don't ever get caught up in this trap: "It's not our job to entertain kids." Maybe not, but if they're not having fun, you're going to lose them. In Deuteronomy 6, the word *teach* means "to cause to learn." My job as a teacher is not over when I give you the information. No, my job as a teacher is over when you learn the information. We are stewards of an hour or more with kids or teenagers and it is up to us to make sure we unpack the message in a way that engages them.

Are you recording what's being presented and evaluating it regularly?

Are you paying attention when kids disengage and adjusting accordingly?

Do communicators start as observers and later receive training, mentoring, and specific encouragement?

GAUGE KEY

0	Not happening
20	Just getting started
40	Making some progress
60	Steadily moving
80	In high gear

Craft core truths into engaging, relevant, and memorable experiences

M6 RELATIONAL EXPERIENCES

Curriculum and content are arranged as catalysts to spark meaningful interaction in the context of consistent groups of peers and a mentor or leader.

No matter what we teach, it will be monumentally less effective unless kids and students know we care about them and believe in them. That's why Paul said, "Speak the truth in love,"[5] because he connected the teaching of truth to the concept of a relationship. When we just speak truth outside of relationship, the truth is sabotaged.

John said Jesus was full of "grace and truth."[6] Both are important. When you create a relational context where there is plenty of grace, you will be surprised at how readily people will respond to the truth. When we surround an individual with a relationship as we unpack truth, something powerful happens.

That's why we believe the role of the large group leader is so critical. Those who work on the front lines with kids or teenagers have the unique function of demonstrating the kind of grace and love that affects a person's ability to process and embrace what is true.

Is there enough time in small groups for a good discussion?

Through vision casting and training, are you emphasizing the small group leader's role as a facilitator and not a teacher?

Do your leaders effectively express truth in the context of grace and relationship?

GAUGE KEY

0	Not happening
20	Just getting started
40	Making some progress
60	Steadily moving
80	In high gear

Refine the Message

APPEALING CONTEXT

Ministries create physical environments that connect with specific age groups and emphasize key elements from the teaching and content.

What is the actual room, the actual setting, where your ministry takes place? What does it look like? What does your facility look like? What does it feel like? This does not mean you have to spend a lot of money to renovate your space. It just means you have to make sure this is an inviting place kids and students will want to be.

Smart leaders know they have to become *environmental specialists*. I have observed a number of leaders around the country who recognize the importance of creating environments that target the tastes and interests of the age groups they are trying to reach. There are so many factors to think through. Apply the senses test. Does it appeal in the way it smells, feels, tastes, sounds, and looks? Are there simple ways to make it more appealing to the season of life you are targeting? Are there distractions that you need to remove? Does the décor you use reinforce what you are teaching? Is there a way to create themes that reinforce a specific series or bottom line you are trying to explain? What can you do to create a place that has appeal to kids or teenagers?

Ask those who specialize in interior design or construction to volunteer their talents, but don't let your environment grow stale. Create something that will complement your message, capture the imagination, and challenge everyone's thinking. Don't fall into the trap of spending an enormous amount of money on something that doesn't reinforce your teaching strategy or on something that will always stay the same. If it is

the same every week for months or years, it will ultimately disappear in the eyes of those in your ministry.

What do you see when you walk through your environments?

What do other people see when they walk your halls and general areas?

How creative are you in leveraging your environments so they help children and students connect to the truth being taught?

Where could you go to find inspiration?

Are you changing often enough so that your décor doesn't become invisible?

GAUGE KEY

0	Not happening
20	Just getting started
40	Making some progress
60	Steadily moving
80	In high gear

Craft core truths into engaging, relevant, and memorable experiences

ACTIVITIES

THE MORE YOU ORE

Stop random parents, volunteers, staff, and children to videotape them answering questions about your message. It might be what they learned this week or maybe the church's mission statement or what is coming up on the calendar. Prepare a promotional video with this funny footage and then conclude the video by showcasing all the different ways they can be "in the know" through signage in the halls, handouts going home, emails, the Web site, TV screens, etc. Go out with the video recorder again in a few weeks, making a big deal that you'll be trying again and that you have prizes. What are the results like this time around? Have fun with it!

KNOW

MOVIE CLIP

One of the best examples of refining your message can be found in Mel Gibson's movie Braveheart.[7] Below are just a few of our favorite lines from this memorable movie. Besides what he said, what did William Wallace do to get his point across? How did his message (and mission) spread through his life, his country, and even his death? What could all this have to do with you and your ministry?

"Would you be willing to trade all the days from this day to that for one chance, just one chance, to come back here and tell our enemies that they may take our lives, but they'll never take our freedom?"

"You think the people of this country exist to provide you with position. I think your position exists to provide those people with freedom, and I go to make sure that they have it."

"Every man dies. Not every man really lives."

ENVIRONMENT
CHECKLIST

☐ Are you using music strategically in your ministry? Don't forget to maximize it in the hallways and during transition times to reinforce your message.

☐ Do you have television screens near the stage, in halls, or in classrooms that can have a key phrase or weekly principle scrolling in an eye-catching way? Don't leave them dark and blank—use them to amplify your message.

☐ Where are the natural focal points or high-traffic areas in your environment where you could write key words for your ministry and post what children are learning today?

☐ What volunteers would be naturals at helping you "set the scene" each week for amazing ministry? They could turn on lights, music, or create slideshows to go with the week's lesson or to highlight upcoming events. You probably have some artsy and handy people who could help you maximize your space and communicate in very low-cost ways. Where could you have them paint key phrases or hang bulletin boards or frames so a volunteer could change the information weekly or monthly? Don't add this to your to-do list, but think about others who could join your team and add their unique gifts in ways other than teaching or leading a small group.

RESOURCING

What resources are going home with parents and leaders so everyone is on the same page? (For example, in our 252 Basics curriculum there's a Refrigerator Door card that summarizes what was discussed at church.)

How easy are you making it for parents to access additional resources if they are interested? (We have a Family Times Virtue kit that helps parents maximize key times in their day, like morning, meals, driving, and bed, for reinforcing spiritual truth and everyday faith.)

For more information, see *Think Orange* Concentrate 8.1 and the next chapter in this workbook about Reactivating the Family.

ORANGE-OMETER

In these spaces, transfer your scores from the component pages earlier in this chapter. Calculate your average score from the seven components and write it in the gauge below.

GAUGE KEY

0	Not happening
20	Just getting started
40	Making some progress
60	Steadily moving
80	In high gear

INTEGRATE STRATEGY

Synchronized Team	S1	[ ]
Designated Leader	S2	[ ]
Consistent Meetings	S3	[ ]
Common Language	S4	[ ]
Clear Wins	S5	[ ]
Strategic Programs	S6	[ ]
Systematic Training	S7	[ ]

REFINE THE MESSAGE

Strategic Teaching	M1	[ ]
Relevant Environments	M2	[ ]
Synchronized Content	M3	[ ]
Focused Truth	M4	[ ]
Engaging Presentation	M5	[ ]
Relational Experiences	M6	[ ]
Appealing Context	M7	[ ]

YOUR VALUE HERE

YOUR VALUE HERE

REACTIVATE THE FAMILY		ELEVATE COMMUNITY		LEVERAGE INFLUENCE	
Compelling Vision	F1	Church-Wide Focus	C1	Strategic Service	I1
Pro-Family Culture	F2	Invested Leaders	C2	Repeated Opportunities	I2
Parental Support	F3	Consistent Relationships	C3	Intentional Apprenticeship	I3
Family Experiences	F4	Family Reinforcement	C4	Targeted Studies	I4
Milestone Emphasis	F5	Graduated System	C5	Global Involvement	I5
Effective Family Time	F6	Spiritual Priorities	C6	Personalized Mission	I6
Community-Wide Focus	F7	Personal Faith	C7	Redemptive Purpose	I7

0 20 40 60 80
YOUR VALUE HERE

0 20 40 60 80
YOUR VALUE HERE

0 20 40 60 80
YOUR VALUE HERE

TWO
COMBINED
INFLUENCES BUILD
AN EVERYDAY FAITH.

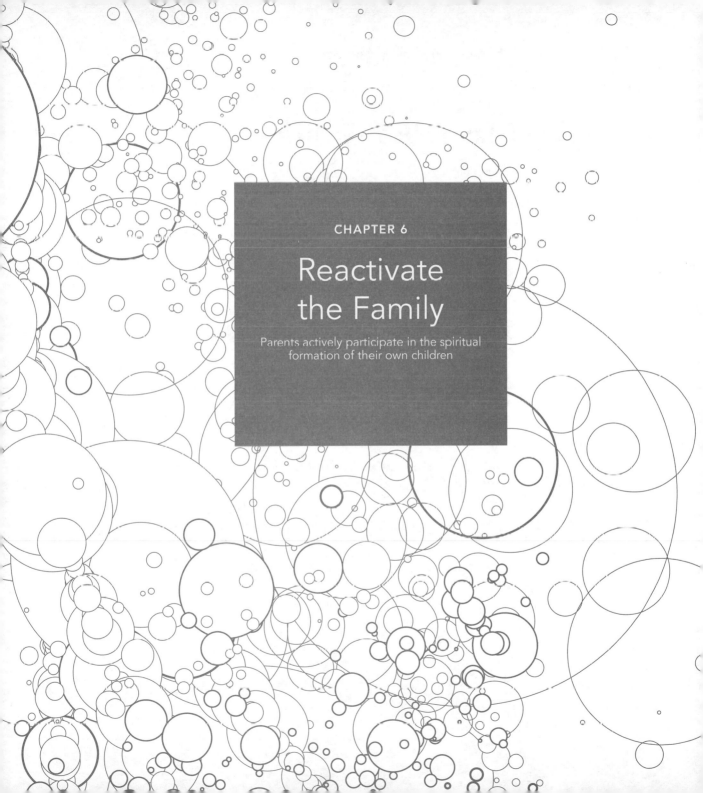

CHAPTER 6

Reactivate the Family

Parents actively participate in the spiritual
formation of their own children

CHAPTER 6
REACTIVATE THE FAMILY

PARENTS ACTIVELY PARTICIPATE IN THE SPIRITUAL FORMATION OF THEIR OWN CHILDREN
Two combined influences build an everyday faith

WHEN WE DON'T REACTIVATE THE FAMILY

Parents tend to abdicate to the church their responsibility to be spiritual leaders.

Parents miss weekly opportunities to connect relationally and spiritually with their kids.

The church forfeits its potential to have greater influence on kids' and students' lives.

Key truths are never synchronized, so churches and homes don't teach the same thing.

The biblical design to influence a child's spiritual and moral formation is never applied.

Churches miss opportunities to meet a critical need in the lives of unchurched parents in their communities.

Students grow up with a view or model of faith that fits into Sunday but not into their daily lives or families.

WHAT ELSE HAPPENS WHEN WE DON'T REACTIVATE THE FAMILY?

JACK-O-LANTERNS
How are you engaging families?

Most families love Halloween. Right or wrong, something about October 31 stirs the imagination of children and engages the hearts of parents. Watch your neighborhood closely this fall.

Listen to the laughter.
Take a look at the generosity.
Taste the sugar.
Feel the energy.
See the glow in the children's eyes.
Notice the parents walking with their kids.
And observe how families connect with other families.
It seems kind of ... magical.

WHY CAN'T CHURCH BE MORE LIKE THAT?
Why can't the church create the kind of atmosphere for families that captures their imaginations and incites a relational revival in their homes? It can, if you think Orange. Halloween Orange! No, I am not endorsing anything, just observing. What if you started thinking differently about the family? Better yet, what if you started acting differently toward parents? Has it ever occurred to you that how you relate to parents may influence how you reactivate the family? By "reactivate the family," we simply mean the way you help parents actively participate in the spiritual formation of their own children.

Get your juices flowing. In the Introduction to *Think Orange*, we talked about how an innovative dad dreamed big to combine family time with an amusement park and media to create the phenomenon we now call Disney. What other leaders, organizations, events, or holidays can you think of that show they value or cater to families? What products or services do they provide? What keeps families coming back for more?

NOTES

SPIRITUAL LEADERSHIP
If you're going to help a parent know how to be a spiritual leader, then you should tell a parent what that phrase actually means. As church leaders, we are notorious for using phrases that have been passed down to us, but we have never stopped to ask what those phrases mean. If you were to send me an email with a clear definition of spiritual leadership, what would it be? Have you ever written one? Church leaders are in a great position to define it in terms that are practical and possible. I am convinced that most parents feel inadequate when they hear the term, and as a result, they are not sure it's something they can do.

Explain what your church and ministry is communicating about family:

verbally in your worship service, programs, and classes

on printed pieces like flyers, postcards, emails, and posters

nonverbally through your environment and setup (the quality and quantity of space, facilities, and resources)

Start thinking about the family and what it takes to create the kind of shared experience that results in quality time for parents and kids. What would happen, for example, if you started acting like what happens at home might be more important than what happens at church? What if you decided that one common goal throughout your children's and student ministries would be to enlist parents to reach their own kids? But be careful. There is a critical difference between trying to complement the family and actually partnering with the family.

Only one out of five parents who attend church say they have ever been contacted by their church to discuss their responsibility to influence their children spiritually.[1]

Why is it that so many parents coming back to church claim that the church has not really helped them lead their kids spiritually? Maybe it's because the church has been programmed to only think in terms of what the church traditionally does. We don't really know how to partner with parents. Our programming and resources are built around the roughly forty hours per year we have with kids in our ministries.

How do you equip parents so they know how to partner with you and lead their families spiritually? How do you make it practical and possible for them to be the spiritual heroes in their homes?

NOTES

GIVE PARENTS HOPE

Some of you are in a better position to influence families than many parenting experts. Assuming that you believe in the importance of family, you have a decision to make about your approach to parents:

You can decide that most parents will probably never change.

You can challenge parents to an idealistic and unattainable standard.

OR

You can choose to believe that most parents, regardless of their baggage, have the desire and capacity to improve.

Make it your goal to convince parents of the following:

God is at work telling a story of restoration and redemption through your family. Never buy into the myth that you need to become the "right" kind of parent before God can use you in your children's lives. Instead, learn to cooperate with whatever God desires to do in your heart today so your children will have a front-row seat to the grace and goodness of God.

How do you *show* that you believe what happens at home is more important than what happens at church? Brainstorm all the different platforms (places, classes, events) or ways (email, bulletin, newsletter) you can get this message out to *all* the parents in your church, over and over again.

NOTES

LEVELS OF PARTNERSHIP WITH PARENTS

All parents are partners with your ministry, but they may be partnering with you at different levels. These four levels help clarify how parents are already partnering so you can move them toward a strategic goal.

AWARE (having perception of a situation)
These parents are concerned about a particular situation or development. These parents are outside the church but open to it, and they're interested in becoming better parents because they genuinely care about their families.

INVOLVED (occupied with activity)
These parents have a basic or entry-level relationship with the church. Even if it's just bringing their kids to church, these parents are taking steps to influence their kids spiritually.

Aware and Involved parents have a lot of untapped potential. Our goal is to move them on to becoming more engaged parents. What specific things are you doing to be able to follow up with Aware/Involved parents, and how are you starting to partner with them and communicate what this looks like from their first visit?

NOTES

INVESTED (devote one's time to a particular undertaking)

These parents proactively devote time and energy to partnering with the church. They understand and value the strategy of your ministry. They are in community with other Christians and can help you in key leadership roles and encouraging other parents.

Invested parents are crucial to your church and ministry because they are the most bought-in and are usually very connected to others. The key is not to take them for granted while making sure they understand the entire strategy, including partnering with the unchurched.

How and when do you follow up and take time to get feedback and cast vision to the Invested parents? (NOTE: Some of your biggest critics or most vocal parents have the potential to be Invested and to be key leaders if you will take the time to explain how all the pieces fit together.)

NOTES

ENGAGED (commit with energy)

These parents are committed to partnering with the church. They are growing in their relationships with God and assume some responsibility for spiritual leadership in the home. They represent a wide spectrum of diverse stages of faith and experience. Remember, the parents who will engage in small ways can make a big difference in the lives of their kids and teenagers.

After a decade in family ministry and several years of creating resources, we keep running into the myth that it's our goal is to get every parent invested. But this isn't true, and it will set you and your team up to feel discouraged and overwhelmed. The focus of your effort as leaders is to help those who are aware and involved to at least become engaged.

The goal is not to engage parents to do everything, but to engage them to do something more.

You believe in family. *But do you believe in parents?* If you do, then ...

1 **Act like every parent is your partner.** I'm not sure we can lead families to see the bigger picture of God's love and restoration if we don't see it ourselves.

2 **Act like every parent can be a better parent.** The idea behind engaging parents into an integrated strategy of the church is built around the belief that what happens at home is more important than what happens at church.

For a great illustration about how we don't set people up to succeed even though they really do want to be better, refer back to *Think Orange* (page 169), and read my story about the woman I met on a plane and her experience with her husband wanting to change.

3 **Act like every parent will do something.** Make sure parents walk away not only motivated but also equipped. They need to know what to do next. We need to provide a very clear next step that changes the rhythm in their homes so they can build an everyday faith.

4 **Act like every parent you meet is coming to your church this Sunday.** Are you ready? You need to be a good steward of your influence (like you are with your time, finances, facilities, and resources). Thinking Orange is thinking smarter. If you want the greatest possible spiritual impact, you have to consider the home in the equation.

Carey Nieuwhof is a senior pastor from Canada who has been a proactive Orange thinker in the Toronto area. He had an Orange epiphany a few years ago as he was preparing to speak on a Sunday morning. "As I was thinking about the parents who lived in the community around our church, something dawned on me. They don't lie in bed at night wondering about the topic I will speak about on Sunday. They don't even lie in bed at night thinking about God. They lie in bed thinking mostly about their kids."

Parents don't parent annually or seasonally. If they come to your church, they need help leading their kids spiritually *right now*. Look at your calendar. If a new parent showed up this Sunday, how long would they have to wait to get help spiritually influencing their children? Currently, how often do you get in the same room with parents? What can you give them that first time that will set you up for a better partnership and great expectations of what's to come? What resources could you have ready and waiting? Don't

think about only printed or packaged materials. How could you leverage the web and media?

NOTES

We need a plan for families that is more encompassing than elite, more organic than programmed, more flexible than rigid. One that can give parents who are in different places in the spiritual spectrum a sense of direction and hope.

INFLUENCING PARENTS

When parents show up at church, they are often asking silent questions we must answer. To begin looking at parents through a different filter, imagine that every time a parent walks through the door, he or she is asking you to do three things:

1 **Give me the plan.** Most parents are parenting reactively, yet many of them desire to be proactive. They want a plan that will give them a system of support, consistent influence, and a steady flow of relevant information. In essence, what they need from the church is a partner.

2 **Show me how it works.** Parents need to be influences as much as children do, and they desire to be engaged in the process in a way that prompts them to take the best next step. Church leadership has the potential to challenge them collectively and give them a network of families to connect with personally.

3 **Tell me what to do today.** If we are going to truly partner with parents, we have to give them specific instructions or resources to use this week. Sometimes parents have a lack of vision, but often they just don't know where to start. Give parents a map and a schedule. (Refer back to *Think Orange* [page 176] for what Malcolm Gladwell discovered about this in his book The Tipping Point.)

We recognized these silent questions from parents years ago and in response created a resource we call the FamilyTimes Virtue Pack, which serves as a "map" and a schedule for parents to use. These Virtue Packs give parents conversation starters and activities to use once a week at strategic times.

FAMILY TIMES
Based on Deuteronomy 6:7, we believe these are the four key times all families can leverage to build the faith of their children:

"Impress [these commands] on your children. Talk about them when you sit at home and when you walk along the road, when you lie down and when you get up."

MEAL TIME
When You Sit at Home
Focused discussion as a teacher to establish core values

DRIVE TIME
When You Walk along the Road
Informal dialogue as a friend to help your child interpret life

BED TIME
When You Lie Down
Intimate conversation as a counselor to listen to the heart of your child

MORNING TIME
When You Get Up
Encouraging words as a coach who gives a sense of value and instills purpose

How do you measure successful parenting? As a church, what are you setting as the standard or ideal? Now flip the question. How are *you* measuring *your* success in partnering with parents? What does your definition of success look and feel like as a church leader?

NOTES

Remember it's not our job to impress parents with what we know about God and about children, and it's not their role to impress their children or anyone else with their ability to parent. Our role is to impress on children the love and character of God.

I'm convinced one of the best ways to stimulate the rhythm of the family and build an everyday faith is to create frequent shared experiences for the whole family.

Over a decade ago, I was on a team that created and started one of the first weekly family experiences in the country. The premise was simple. We felt like we needed to put parents and kids together in a shared environment on a frequent basis. Instead of putting children in a service designed for adults, we flipped the concept: We put adults in a service designed for kids. We hosted and produced this program, KidStuf, every week, and it became an integral part of our strategy. When we first brainstormed the idea and got advice from other children's directors around the country, they discouraged the idea. We were told that any environment that went from kindergarten to fifth grade and included parents would span too many ages.

We almost gave up on the idea until a movie came out that year that reinforced the concept for us—The Lion King. At the time, my children were eleven, nine, seven, and five. As I sat with them I realized there were some pretty talented people who had mastered the art of creating a family experience. They were proving the church experts wrong. Halfway through the movie it was obvious that Disney's writers were scripting on two levels. They had included lines that would keep all ages in the audience engaged. I would chuckle at a one-liner from Whoopi Goldberg's laughing hyena character, and my five-year-old would eye me like she didn't understand what was funny. When she giggled at something Simba did, I rolled my eyes. My son was intrigued with the elephant graveyard. Everyone in my family responded to the part that had been designed for them. We shared an incredible experience together.

As we talked about our favorite scenes on the way home, I had an epiphany. I thought, "Why can't church be like this?" A few months later, we started KidStuf in an elementary school cafeteria. We had a black backdrop painted with the KidStuf name, a couple of singers, two hosts, an actor, and a camcorder I purchased from a big box electronics store. Today, churches around the country are producing quarterly, monthly, and weekly family experiences. Some are production-driven, others are large groups-driven, some are holiday-oriented, but every family experience is built on the same idea: It's not what happens during the family experiences that is most important but what happens between them.

Shortly after we began KidStuf, a CEO who had been attending with his daughter came to me and said, "I have been attending KidStuf for a few weeks, and it's really my first experience with a church. My daughter has started asking me questions about 'spiritual stuff' and I was wondering if I could meet with you so I can figure out what to tell her." It was that day that I decided I would look at all parents assuming they wanted to be better parents.

I wish someone had talked to me when my son turned sixteen and said, "Okay, your son is about to turn sixteen and this is what you can expect." My wife and I didn't have a major argument until our son turned sixteen. Decisions were being made at warp speed so, because of some overarching issues, we ended up making a lot of decisions independently, rather than together. Things were moving so fast we couldn't stay on the same page with all the changes. But these changes are predictable, and you can help parents prepare for them.

FAMILY AS A PRIORITY

"There is no doubt that it is around the family and the home that all the greatest virtues, the most dominating virtues of human society, are created, strengthened, and maintained."
—Winston Churchill[2]

Family shapes us.
Family connects us.
Family influences our stories.
Who is shaping your story?

The loop of engagement is a balance of action best described like a yo-yo. The potential power or source is at the top. There's a definite pattern: Up to get energy, down to spin the message and demonstrate the principle. All the family events and initiatives are on one string instead of several—this prevents tangles.

Questions to ask yourself and your team:

Where do your families get their energy?

What kinds of environments or resources work to give your families energy?

What information do they need to keep them on track?

How frequently do they need to get energy from the source?

When it comes to your programs or events, how often do you need to send them back to the top?

What programs should be weekly, monthly, or occasionally?

Are there any programs or events that are more draining to the church leadership or families than they are energy-giving?

As we continue to dialogue about how we as church leaders partner with families, we don't want to forget that many of us have families of our own. For a personal story about me and my kids, read pages 182 and 183 of *Think Orange* to see how this has played out in my own family. These are the values we keep in front of us as parents and want to model for other parents watching.

FAMILY VALUES
Many leaders are fighting for their definitions of "family values," but often they have forgotten what it means

to value their families. A closer look at Deuteronomy 6:4–7 reminds us to stay focused and keep trying.

IMAGINE THE END
Focus your priorities on what matters most.

FIGHT FOR THE HEART
Communicate in a style that gives the relationship value.

MAKE IT PERSONAL
Put yourself first when it comes to personal growth.

CREATE A RHYTHM
Increase the quantity of quality time you spend together.

WIDEN THE CIRCLE
Pursue strategic relationships for your kids.

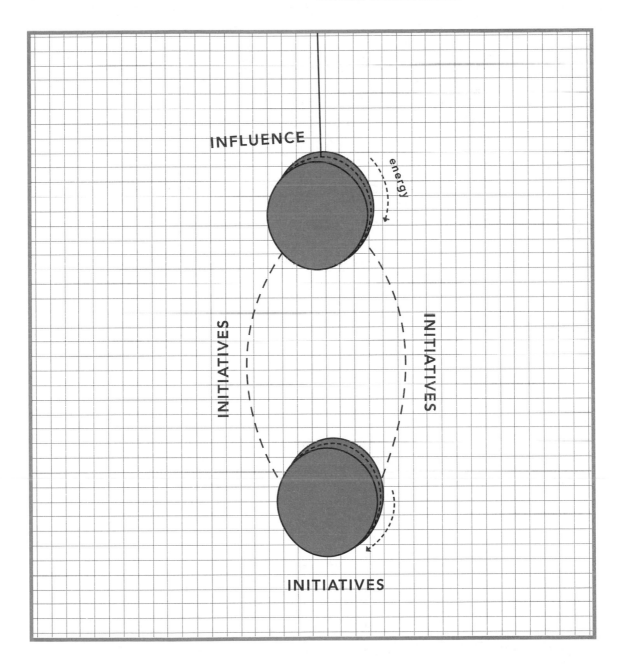

FAMILY

THE SEVEN COMPONENTS TO REACTIVATE THE FAMILY
PARENTS ACTIVELY PARTICIPATE IN THE SPIRITUAL FORMATION OF THEIR OWN CHILDREN

An untapped potential exists when we simply decide we are going to be more family-oriented. We may say we are "family-friendly," but when we look at our programming and the way we schedule events and arrange the pieces, is it evident that family is really a priority? These characteristics will help you evaluate how deep your commitment to family really is.

These seven components will help clarify what it can look like when a church is becoming Orange. Use them as points of reference to gauge how well you are doing in each area.

F1. COMPELLING VISION

F2. PRO-FAMILY CULTURE

F3. PARENTAL SUPPORT

F4. FAMILY EXPERIENCES

F5. MILESTONE EMPHASIS

F6. EFFECTIVE FAMILY TIME

F7. COMMUNITY-WIDE FOCUS

COMPELLING VISION

Church leaders establish a clear expectation that parents should assume the primary responsibility of leading their children morally and spiritually.

Parents need to understand the vision you have for their kids and their families. Articulate it, craft it, and simplify it so every parent understands it and every leader can communicate it. Demonstrate that family is important by the way your church prioritizes relationships among families, even down to the way your volunteers model marriage and parenting.

Parents can't partner with you unless they understand what you want them to see. You need to be able to stand in front of parents, with a common language, and on whatever platform, and explain easily where you're going and where, together, you're taking their children and students.

Does your church's lead communicator present a family series once a year?

What opportunities are already built into your culture to cast vision?

What are some features or promotional spots you can do in the service to cast vision?

How can you create compelling and clever graphics (in print, on the walls, on the Web) to communicate the partnership between families and the church?

GAUGE KEY

0	Not happening
20	Just getting started
40	Making some progress
60	Steadily moving
80	In high gear

Parents actively participate in the spiritual formation of their own children

F2 PRO-FAMILY CULTURE

Staff establishes a pro-family church culture by communicating strategically, modeling personal priorities, and reducing competing programming.

When someone looks at your church calendar, does it look like you've made space within it for families to be families? As you declutter your calendar, focus on high-impact events that celebrate the concept of family and church partnerships. How do your staff members who have families model the personal priority of family? Andy Stanley's book *Choosing to Cheat* revolutionized our perspective on practical ways for staff and leaders to demonstrate a family priority. The greatest gift Andy gave to those of us on staff was permission to put our families first.

When you look at your church, do the actions of the leadership team and the style of ministry reflect a family intention? Does your senior pastor speak about family on a regular basis? Even in your ministry to single adults, is family promoted as a positive next step for those who are moving into another stage of life?

How do you encourage your key leaders and staff to protect their family time?

Do you intentionally create opportunities to celebrate the family?

Is your church calendar overscheduled with competing programs for families, kids, and parents?

Have you identified staff and key leadership who are positive models for marriage and family?

Are the children of your key leaders and staff excited by the activity in the church with their parents, or do they resent it?

GAUGE KEY

0	Not happening
20	Just getting started
40	Making some progress
60	Steadily moving
80	In high gear

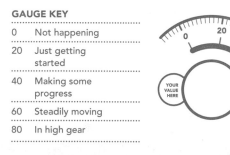

Reactivate the Family

F3

PARENTAL SUPPORT

Parents are systematically encouraged to develop critical skills so they can have a positive influence and healthy relationships with their children through group or training experiences.

Most parents desire to network and connect with other parents who are going through the same season-of-life issues they are. Parents who show up at your church want to make sure they're doing all this the right way. Sometimes, that means a parent who is a little further along saying, "This is all going to work out."

Small groups are critical. reThink is currently working on small group studies that help parents get together with other parents to talk about strategy. This way, they can participate in what is happening in the church and encourage each other to move through this process. Parents need to know where they can go and what they can do in times of trouble or crisis.

Are there small group studies or parenting classes where you could share tools and a plan?

Do you strategically use an Internet site to communicate vision and share the plan?

Are you leveraging key events or opportunities to give parents specific things to do at home to interact with kids?

GAUGE KEY

0	Not happening
20	Just getting started
40	Making some progress
60	Steadily moving
80	In high gear

Parents actively participate in the spiritual formation of their own children

F4

FAMILY EXPERIENCES

Consistent family experiences are created within the church as a catalyst for meaningful interaction at home.

For too long, the church has segregated parents from their kids. So for children we make sure parents have a regular experience together with their kids. It allows the kids to walk away and talk about the same thing with their parents that they're discussing in church. We think this looks different for different age groups.

When it comes to the student ministry, we try to get the small group leaders and parents together in very nonthreatening and encouraging ways. We think every camp, retreat, or trip is an opportunity for ministry leaders to engage with parents. This can be done in a short meeting that explains to parents what will be happening with that event. There are probably several activities already built into your calendar that could be leveraged for that purpose.

One of the ways we've fostered this is a series we created for our XP3 student curriculum. The series is called "The Good Fight," and the study shows students why it's important for them to fight for their relationships with their parents. As part of this, we bring the parents in and speak to them separately, so the parents and students are on the same page. That's just one way to create a family experience that brings mom and dad together with their sons and daughters.

Do environments already exist where adults and their kids have a shared experience?

How often do you create an opportunity for parents to participate in a challenge with their sons and daughters?

Do you capitalize on natural family times, like holidays?

Do you specifically target and work on the family relationship?

GAUGE KEY

0	Not happening
20	Just getting started
40	Making some progress
60	Steadily moving
80	In high gear

Reactivate the Family

<table>
<tr><td>**F5**</td><td># MILESTONE EMPHASIS
Parents are actively involved in key events that mark critical passages for growth of children.</td></tr>
</table>

In every year of a high school student's life, that student passes a milestone. Belonging is a real issue for ninth graders. For tenth graders, it's freedom. Eleventh graders are facing identity questions, while high school seniors are determining their future direction. With every milestone issue, small group leaders help their students talk about it and unpack it so everyone—including parents—can be prepared.

As we go through the seasons of life with our children, we have a tendency to disengage as our young people become teenagers. *Too many parents check out exactly when they need to be checking in.* We need leaders who will say, "As your son or daughter moves toward independence, it's essential that you reengage and redefine your place in their lives so you continue to have relevant influence."

By assisting in defining and celebrating key transitions with parents and families at certain milestones, you help set them up for success.

Have you identified the core issue for each age group?

How can you prepare parents to understand these major concerns and help guide their responses to them?

Do parents, children, and students anticipate the milestone markers or celebrations?

How does this process build generation after generation?

GAUGE KEY

0	Not happening
20	Just getting started
40	Making some progress
60	Steadily moving
80	In high gear

Parents actively participate in the spiritual formation of their own children

F6 — EFFECTIVE FAMILY TIME

Curriculums and resources are designed so core truths can be taught at home and at church in a synchronized effort.

This is the goal: How do we reactivate families so they can spend more quality time together? Our goal isn't to convince the parent to do everything right, but if we can get them to focus on at least a few ways to have more effective family time, we've made a difference.

Sometimes we overthink what it takes. But what it takes is pretty simple. If the dad of the seventh-grade boy who has never prayed with him prays with him, it will make a greater impact than anything else in that boy's life. Get every parent to do a little something more.

So many times, we don't extend our creative energy to helping parents have better relationships with their children and students. What can the church do to make this kind of an impression in the lives of families we reach?

What key resources do you provide for parents to take home to synchronize with what is taught?

What indicators are you looking for to see if families are using some of the resources at home?

Do you have a focus group or other way to gather insight from participating families?

GAUGE KEY

0	Not happening
20	Just getting started
40	Making some progress
60	Steadily moving
80	In high gear

Reactivate the Family

COMMUNITY-WIDE FOCUS

Experiences and accessibility are made available for those who might not normally be comfortable in a church setting.

Many of the families we most need to reach are the least likely to come to our churches. How do we reach the families next door? We must care for those families who are on the periphery of our churches but just don't know how to be a family. Begin to look at all the parents you meet in your community not as prospects, but as partners. Figure out how you can help them be better parents. Every parent wants to do this.

Don't just think about the parents inside your church. Constantly ask yourself, "How can we leverage our experience to reach families outside the church?" I could give you story after story after story of parents who became Christians because their children participated in what we were doing. Don't write off your non-Christian parents. I think every parent wants to do better, and every parent wants to do something more. These parents are looking for some kind of hope, any kind of hope. Who offers that more than the church?

Would a nonattending family easily understand how to participate and connect?

Do families that already attend feel great about inviting those outside the church to come?

Have you discovered how to be present and accessible in the extended community?

Do those outside the church have a positive impression after leaving your church or ministry?

GAUGE KEY

0	Not happening
20	Just getting started
40	Making some progress
60	Steadily moving
80	In high gear

Parents actively participate in the spiritual formation of their own children

ACTIVITIES

ONE OF THE BEST EXAMPLES OF REACTIVATING FAMILIES CAN BE FOUND IN THE MOVIE *THE INCREDIBLES*.[3] IN THE FIRST SCENE DEPICTED ON THE NEXT PAGE, HELEN (THE WIFE) IS DESPERATE FOR HER HUSBAND, BOB, TO ENGAGE WITH THEIR FAMILY INSTEAD OF THINKING BACK ON HIS GLORY DAYS. BY THE LAST SCENE, IT'S EASY TO TELL THAT HE'S MADE A HUGE DISCOVERY.

MOVIE CLIP

HOW IS THIS COLORFUL, ANIMATED FAMILY LIKE THE FAMILIES IN YOUR CHURCH OR MINISTRY?

BEFORE SCENE

DASH: SHE'D EAT IF WE WERE HAVING TONYLOAF.

VIOLET: THAT'S IT! [jumps at Dash]

HELEN: BOTH OF YOU SIT DOWN! [Dash runs around the table, hitting Violet as he passes her, until Violet makes a force field to stop him]

DASH: HEY! NO FORCE FIELDS!

VIOLET: YOU STARTED IT!

HELEN: [grabs Dash and puts him on his seat] YOU SIT DOWN!
[grabs Violet and puts her in her seat]

HELEN: YOU SIT DOWN! VIOLET!
[Dash and Violet run under the table to fight, dragging Helen against the table]

BOB: [reading newspaper in the other room] "SIMON J. PALADINO, LONGTIME ADVOCATE OF SUPERHERO RIGHTS, IS MISSING" ... GAZER BEAM ...

HELEN: BOB! IT'S TIME TO ENGAGE! DO SOMETHING! DON'T JUST STAND THERE; I NEED YOU TO INTERVENE!

BOB: INTERVENE?
[picks up table]

BOB: OKAY, I'M INTERVENING!

AFTER SCENE

BOB: [Everyone is trapped in Syndrome's containment unit] I'M SORRY. THIS IS MY FAULT. I'VE BEEN A LOUSY FATHER, BLIND TO WHAT I HAVE. SO OBSESSED WITH BEING UNDERVALUED THAT I UNDERVALUED ALL OF YOU. [While Bob is talking, Violet frees herself using her force field]

DASH: UM, DAD ...

HELEN: SHH, DON'T INTERRUPT.

BOB: SO ... CAUGHT UP IN THE PAST THAT I ... YOU ARE MY GREATEST ADVENTURE, AND I ALMOST MISSED IT. I SWEAR, I'M GONNA GET US OUT OF THIS SAFELY IF I ...

VIOLET: [At the control panel] WELL, I THINK DAD HAS MADE SOME EXCELLENT PROGRESS TODAY, BUT I THINK IT'S TIME WE WIND DOWN NOW.

[She frees them by hitting a green button]

COPY THIS ONE OR CREATE YOUR OWN DRAWING OF A LARGE YO-YO AND WRITE DOWN DIFFERENT PROGRAMS, EVENTS, AND RESOURCES ON INDIVIDUAL POST-IT NOTES. GIVE EACH ONE A SCORE BASED ON HOW MUCH ENERGY YOU THINK IT GIVES FAMILIES. THINK ABOUT HOW LONG THAT ENERGY LASTS—IS IT A QUICK HIT OR MORE SUSTAINED?

Arrange all the Post-its on the yo-yo drawing and leave it up for a time after you've talked about this with your team. Go back to your focus group or key Engaged or Invested parents and see what they think. Remember to be willing to stop doing things!

CLUE FINDER

Look back at your calendar, budget, and staff/volunteer structure. What percentage of your resources [time, money, staff, etc.] is focused on reactivating the family?

FAMILY EXPERIENCES

What experiences, programs, or events do you currently have in place that put parents and children in the same room? Where and how often do these family experiences occur?

(ex., Celebrating spiritual milestones like baptism or baby dedication, Christmas, or Easter)

_____

_____

_____

_____

_____

_____

_____

GET PERSONAL

PICTURE THE FACES AND FAMILIES OF PARENTS THAT SEEM TO FALL UNDER THESE **4** DIFFERENT LEVELS: AWARE, INVOLVED, INVESTED, ENGAGED. PUT THEIR NAMES ON POST-IT NOTES IF THAT HELPS KEEP THEM IN YOUR MIND.

ARE YOU MAKING THE STEP SEEM ***TOO BIG*** FOR AWARE OR INVOLVED PARENTS? ARE YOU CHALLENGING INVESTED PARENTS TO LEAD WITH YOU? WHAT **SMALL**, **PRACTICAL**, AND **POSSIBLE** STEPS CAN YOU REGULARLY COMMUNICATE INSTEAD OF ASKING THEM TO DO TOO MUCH ALL AT ONCE?

ORANGE-OMETER

In these spaces, transfer your scores from the component pages earlier in this chapter. Calculate your average score from the seven components and write it in the gauge below.

GAUGE KEY

0	Not happening
20	Just getting started
40	Making some progress
60	Steadily moving
80	In high gear

INTEGRATE STRATEGY

Synchronized Team	S1	
Designated Leader	S2	
Consistent Meetings	S3	
Common Language	S4	
Clear Wins	S5	
Strategic Programs	S6	
Systematic Training	S7	

REFINE THE MESSAGE

Strategic Teaching	M1	
Relevant Environments	M2	
Synchronized Content	M3	
Focused Truth	M4	
Engaging Presentation	M5	
Relational Experiences	M6	
Appealing Context	M7	

YOUR VALUE HERE

0   20   40   60   80

YOUR VALUE HERE

0   20   40   60   80

REACTIVATE THE FAMILY		ELEVATE COMMUNITY		LEVERAGE INFLUENCE	
Compelling Vision	F1	Church-Wide Focus	C1	Strategic Service	I1
Pro-Family Culture	F2	Invested Leaders	C2	Repeated Opportunities	I2
Parental Support	F3	Consistent Relationships	C3	Intentional Apprenticeship	I3
Family Experiences	F4	Family Reinforcement	C4	Targeted Studies	I4
Milestone Emphasis	F5	Graduated System	C5	Global Involvement	I5
Effective Family Time	F6	Spiritual Priorities	C6	Personalized Mission	I6
Community-Wide Focus	F7	Personal Faith	C7	Redemptive Purpose	I7

YOUR VALUE HERE   0   20   40   60   80

YOUR VALUE HERE   0   20   40   60   80

YOUR VALUE HERE   0   20   40   60   80

TWO
COMBINED
INFLUENCES
INCREASE
THE ODDS.

Elevate Community

Everyone is connected to a caring leader
and a consistent group of peers

CHAPTER 7

ELEVATE COMMUNITY

EVERYONE IS CONNECTED TO A CARING LEADER AND A CONSISTENT GROUP OF PEERS
Two combined influences increase the odds

WHEN WE DON'T ELEVATE COMMUNITY

Parents feel alone in trying to have moral and spiritual influence with their children.

The church is characterized by superficial relationships.

We tend to reproduce a generation of Christians who can't develop authentic relationships.

Key truths are never synchronized, so churches and homes don't teach the same thing.

Students tend to pursue counsel and advice in unhealthy relationships.

Productions or programs are positioned as the answer.

Leaders fail to discover their potential to make a significant investment in someone's life.

WHAT ELSE HAPPENS WHEN WE DON'T ELEVATE COMMUNITY?

BASKETBALL
How are you connecting kids and students to leaders?

Many people know that in 1891 Dr. James Naismith invented the game of basketball. Not a lot of people, however, know about the contribution of Tony Hinkle in the late 1950s. Hinkle made it easier for spectators and players to see the ball by making it orange. Today, basketball is the only sport that has an official orange ball.

Any winning team has to meet on a frequent basis to practice plays, learn strategies, and increase personal skills. The right coach can make all the difference. The next time you watch a basketball game, focus on the head coach. The coach moves along the sidelines with the players, giving constant instructions.

Ask high school basketball players. They will tell you that most of the time they never hear the echoes of the gym floor, the roar of the crowd, or the shouts of their own parents. They only hear the solitary voice of the coach.

SPIRITUAL COACHING
A time arrives in a young person's life when he or she seems to care more about what another adult says than what his or her own parents say. That's why it's important to start early in pointing those kids to grown-ups whose voices you trust and value.

When we talk about elevating community, we are talking about strategically placing coaches in the lives of our children and teenagers. Growing up in this generation requires some pretty significant relationships. Children and students need the skills to navigate through some difficult obstacles, and they need the right voices to give them wise direction.

If you look back over your own life, you will probably notice that certain individuals stand out over time because of the impact they had in your life. When churches embrace this principle, they help parents by meeting the needs of children and teenagers to have older mentors. One of the greatest gifts your church can give any parent or child is a consistent network of leaders and friends, outside the family, who are there to help both parents and kids win.

Everyone needs to be believed in by someone, and everyone needs to belong somewhere. True community provides both.

Read more about my personal experience with this and my daughter Hannah in *Think Orange*, starting on page 185.

Which do you think comes first—believing or belonging? Can you think of specific stories of people for whom this is true? Which order does your church emphasize? Believe first, then we'll put you in a group. Or, we'll connect you to a group, thinking that might help you believe.

NOTES

COMMUNITY MATTERS

In a survey of one thousand young people from ages eighteen to thirty, researchers found, "Teens who had at least one adult from church make a significant time investment in their lives … were more likely to keep attending church. More of those who stayed in church—by a margin of 46 percent to 28 percent—said five or more adults had invested time with them personally and spiritually."[1]

How do we earn "relational change" in the pockets of children and teenagers? What do you think a significant time investment looks like from their perspective? If you looked at your plan or system right now, how many adults will invest time in each of the teenagers at your church?

NOTES

Researcher Scott McConnell says the presence of adult mentors is one key to solving the dropout rate for the 70 percent of teens who graduate and walk away from the church: "Investment time in young people lives out the love of Jesus Christ in a tangible way. It proves that a young person belongs at church. It can help connect the dots to help a teen integrate their faith into their life. And it gives the teen a connection to church after graduation when many of their peers are no longer around."[2]

True community happens when everyone is connected to a caring leader and a consistent group of peers.

Listen to all the things that can happen when we create this sense of community:

Parents feel supported, not alone, in trying to have moral and spiritual influence with their children.

The church is characterized by meaningful and significant relationships, not superficial ones.

We reproduce a generation of Christians who are able to develop authentic relationships easily.

Students will pursue counsel from Christian mentors rather than from unhealthy relationships.

Productions or programs are positioned as a step in a process rather than the whole answer.

Leaders discover their potential to make a lasting investment in someone's life.

When you elevate community, you recognize the need for multiple voices.

When Jesus came to earth, He set the example that life is to be lived in consistent community. Why should we live any other way? We need to intentionally place leaders in the lives of children and students who can partner with parents in the work God is doing.

Think about what a commitment to small group or community in your children's and student ministries would mean. What are the pros and cons of a classroom or master-teacher format compared with a small group mentality? How would a consistent leader and several peers each week make a different impact? What would be your thirty-second elevator pitch for this change in philosophy?

UNCOMMON SENSE
to help them make wise choices
God's point of view and His truth should become the filter for how kids view life and make decisions.

NOSY PARENTS
who know where their kids are spiritually
Kids need parents who will be intentional about spending time together as a family and staying actively involved in their children's spiritual growth.

Think back over your life. Make a quick list or draw a timeline with significant events and individuals who stand out because of their impact and positive influence. How many of them were adults? When you look over this, do you feel really privileged, or do you wish there had been more voices?

Early on at North Point, our Family Ministry team came up with a list of five things that every kid needs. More than a decade later, these things are still true.

THINGS EVERY KID NEEDS

A REALLY BIG GOD
they can trust no matter what
Kids should grow up knowing that God is big enough to handle whatever they may face.

SOMEONE ELSE
who believes what they believe
Kids need friends who will encourage them to grow in their faith.

ANOTHER VOICE
saying the same things parents say
As children grow older it becomes more important to have other adults in their lives as spiritual mentors and leaders.

Over time, community is how people grow. Children learn in the context of relationships—when their lives intersect with the lives of others. They have a better chance of understanding and applying life-changing truth when there are multiple influences in their lives all saying the same thing. For leaders and parents to work together, they need a common language. This is why we at reThink settled on five Faith Skills for leaders, parents, and children to grow in spiritually.

FAITH SKILLS

NAVIGATE THE BIBLE: survey, locate
To learn where they can go to find verses that will help them with specific questions

PERSONALIZE SCRIPTURE: memorize, apply
To remember Scripture when they need it most and apply it in everyday situations

DIALOGUE WITH GOD: public, private
To encourage them to practice talking with God

ARTICULATE YOUR FAITH: share, defend
To be able to discuss and wrestle with what they believe so children and teenagers can make their faith their own

WORSHIP WITH YOUR LIFE: serve, invest
To know how to give back to God and to serve Him in the way they live their everyday lives

When you elevate community, you help kids or students navigate through critical life situations. For a great example of the impact this can have, read one leader's email about what happened when tragedy struck in the life of Brandon and his family on page 192 of *Think Orange*.

> What critical life situations are kids or students in your ministry dealing with right now? What difference could a consistent small group leader and group of peers make in these cases?

NOTES

When you elevate community, you cooperate with how God grows people spiritually. The team that started North Point sat around debating how to help people really grow in their relationships with Christ. So we started telling our stories, recounting the defining moments in our lives when our faith was stretched to a new dimension. Afterward, we looked at our stories and realized that although they were very different, there were similar patterns. It's almost as if God had used the same chords over and over in every one of our lives to write different songs. When you or I or kids or students grow, it is usually because of one or more of the following.

CATALYSTS FOR SPIRITUAL GROWTH
As a leader, your primary role in the lives of others is to leverage what God is already doing to help them grow as Christians. What if you organized your ministries around these five key issues?

LIFE-CHANGING TRUTH
What is your role in teaching or amplifying spiritual truth for them?

SPIRITUAL DISCIPLINES
What can you do to help them develop personal spiritual habits?

PERSONAL MINISTRY
How can you encourage them to establish a personal ministry?

SIGNIFICANT RELATIONSHIPS
How can you be more effective at using your life to influence those you lead? How can you mobilize other leaders to pursue meaningful relationships with children and teenagers?

PIVOTAL CIRCUMSTANCES
What is your responsibility when it comes to crisis or difficult situations in their lives?

When you elevate community, you recruit and nurture a different breed of spiritual leaders. We found that volunteers who knew they would be disconnected from the kids as soon as the day or month was over had a tendency to be inconsistent. When the volunteers were connected relationally to the same kids every week, week after week, their commitment level increased.

When churches bought into the idea that volunteers were inconsistent, their self-fulfilling prophecy fueled unmotivated leaders. By shifting to a model that asked volunteers to be an essential part of authentic community, the leaders felt a sense of connectivity and meaning. They had a meaningful mission.

What is your honest attitude toward recruiting volunteers? Do you come from a *scarcity* or an *abundance* mindset? Are you willing to set up your volunteers to win with clear expectations, resources, and training?

Do you believe that asking *a lot* from your volunteers and being selective about who you plug in where is the key to a solid team of rain-or-shine leaders?

NOTES

When you elevate community, you do something that nothing in culture can match. People assume that part of the reason we were successful at North Point was our budget or that we could create amazing environments. But in the beginning we had very little, so that can't be the whole story. There isn't a church out there that can out-produce Hollywood or Disney. But here's the good news: *Culture can never outdo churches in the way they can create community.*

CREATING COMMUNITY
No matter how much culture tries to mimic community by creating false environments and shallow relationships, culture can never be a consistent, personal presence in the lives of parents and children. Creating community is something every church can do regardless of size or budget simply by placing another consistent adult in the life of every child and student in your ministry. When this happens, children and students know there is a place where they can have a safe and meaningful spiritual discussion with an adult who cares. When that happens, nothing can compete.

What are some creative ways you can show you're investing wholeheartedly in community and elevating relationships? How do you collect stories from your small group leaders and celebrate life change with them? How often do you get together with leaders for training and feedback?

NOTES

Have you or any of your kids ever been with the same coach, teacher, or mentor for several years in a row? What are the benefits of this graduated system? Could you start this approach with your high school small group leaders and work your way to younger groups over time?

NOTES

When you elevate community, it changes everything. Kids subconsciously recognize the value and become adults knowing community is something they need and want.

If you "up the ante" and start recruiting leaders who graduate with their kids, especially as you move toward middle and high school, here's just a short list of all the things you might accomplish:

You recruit a different caliber of leader.

You guarantee that some will connect for four years, and many others will invest for at least a few years.

They discover a different kind of perspective and motivation that comes with a long-term commitment.

It will also change the way you lead strategically. You will prioritize differently. Your focus shifts from *doing more* to *doing things well*. Your main concern will be to find the right kinds of leaders to invest in.

You will look at programs differently—not as one-time or annual experiences. Now every program needs to be a step in the process that moves toward community. This will further change the way you look at your calendar and budget.

Line up in your mind or on paper the different programs that you spend time and resources on. If you knew community was the end goal, what would you stop or change? What is the biggest drain on your budget that isn't really moving leaders and children/students into deeper relationships?

NOTES

When you elevate community, you provide reinforcement to the parent. You are providing their kids or teenagers a safe and trusted place where they can ask difficult questions and get advice from healthy sources.

I make Sam [my son] go [to church] because the youth group leaders know things I don't. They know what teenagers are looking for, and they need adults who have stayed alive and vital, adults they wouldn't mind growing up to be.... And they need total acceptance of who they are, from adults they trust, and to be welcomed in whatever condition life has left them—needy, walled-off, glowering. They want guides, adults who know how to act like adults but with a kid's heart. They want people who will sit with them and talk about the big questions, even if they don't have the answers; adults who won't correct their feelings or pretend not to be afraid. They are looking for adventure, experience, pilgrimages, and thrills. And then they want a home they can return to, where things are stable and welcoming.
–Anne Lamott[3]

When you elevate community, you give parents the gift of community. In *Think Orange*, I give another personal example about when my son turned sixteen and didn't want to talk with me about a girl (you can read more of this story starting on page 201 of *Think Orange*). The exchange leads to a powerful moment in our relationship.

I asked my son, "If you won't tell me, then who will you tell?" And he gave me a name. That name made all the difference in the world because it was a lifelong friend of mine. I knew this friend loved our family, respected me, and had the same values. I didn't have to worry anymore.

If the parents in your ministry asked their sons or daughters, "Who are you going to talk to, if it's not me?" Would they have a name? Would it be someone the parent could trust? Are you putting coaches in children's and students' lives who can be trusted?

NOTES

COMMUNITY

THE SEVEN COMPONENTS TO ELEVATE COMMUNITY
EVERYONE IS CONNECTED TO A CARING LEADER AND CONSISTENT GROUP OF PEERS

While we sometimes target our resources toward a main-event speaker or large group program, the single most important element of your ministry is how you're fostering powerful God-centered relationships for children and students. Doing life together with a leader is what makes the difference, so these are some of the components that will help you measure how effectively you're building these kinds of connections.

These seven components will help clarify what it can look like when a church is becoming Orange. Use them as points of reference to gauge how well you are doing in each area.

C1. CHURCH-WIDE FOCUS

C2. INVESTED LEADERS

C3. CONSISTENT RELATIONSHIPS

C4. FAMILY REINFORCEMENT

C5. GRADUATED SYSTEM

C6. SPIRITUAL PRIORITIES

C7. PERSONAL FAITH

C1 CHURCH-WIDE FOCUS

Programs and volunteers' positions are structured as steps toward the primary goal of experiencing community.

It's important that every small group of children or students has a specific person who leads them. Break down the organization so they have a relational, connecting entity. The structure of your ministry should be built around small groups, not programs or presentation. Too often, we create the bigger experience, then break that down into small groups. Instead, we should offer large group experiences as platforms that usher children and students into real relationships with consistent leaders.

Does everyone generally understand what's meant by the term "community"?

Are you clarifying that "community" means groups meeting consistently?

Is everything the church does seen as a step toward community or groups?

How does each environment ultimately set up community or groups to win?

GAUGE KEY

0	Not happening
20	Just getting started
40	Making some progress
60	Steadily moving
80	In high gear

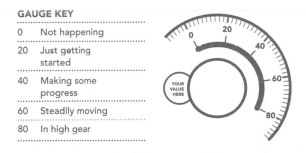

Everyone is connected to a caring leader and consistent group of peers

C2

INVESTED LEADERS

Children and students are organized to meet with a consistent group of peers and a leader who assumes a level of responsibility for their spiritual formation.

Sometimes we think our jobs are to try to get people to participate in our children's or student ministry, when what we're actually trying to do is connect leaders to kids and teenagers relationally. If you're having difficulty recruiting leaders or getting your current leaders to show up, then you don't have invested leaders. When you are invested in someone else's life, it changes your commitment level. As you structure, promote, and nurture your process, it should inspire invested leaders who wouldn't dream of missing time with their kids—because they realize just how important it really is.

Is the small group leader seen as one of the pivotal roles in your ministry?

Is vision clearly cast with regard to the responsibility of the small group leader?

Are staff members organized, trained, and encouraged to emphasize this key role?

GAUGE KEY

0	Not happening
20	Just getting started
40	Making some progress
60	Steadily moving
80	In high gear

Elevate Community

CONSISTENT RELATIONSHIPS

Small groups are valued and championed at every age level as a primary environment to help kids grow spiritually and connect relationally.

Recently we interviewed school counselors and discussed the problems kids face in middle school. The conversation found its way to the intrigue this age group has with gangs. One of the counselors suggested that as kids become teenagers, it becomes more important for them to find their own tribe—they are driven by their need for acceptance and their desire to be a part of something bigger than themselves. I believe kids sometimes respond in a wrong way to a God-created drive—a drive for relationships. God has wired us to need each other. We say it over and over again: It is vitally important to have a place where kids and students know there are people who believe in them, places where they belong. We should be the first to offer kids and teenagers a consistent and safe place to belong, with leaders who believe in their spiritual potential.

Is time spent organizing ministry to make sure relationships aren't economized?

Do you regularly evaluate key environments to see how they're helping community or small groups work?

GAUGE KEY

0	Not happening
20	Just getting started
40	Making some progress
60	Steadily moving
80	In high gear

YOUR VALUE HERE

Everyone is connected to a caring leader and consistent group of peers

C4	**FAMILY REINFORCEMENT**

Parents value small group leaders as partners in teaching and modeling truths to their children, and small group leaders see their roles as assisting and supporting parents.

As a leader, you see your role as one that reinforces the family, even if the family is dysfunctional and the parents aren't doing what they need to do. No matter what, family is still important.

In even marginally effective families, you're able to point out what really works and make sure students don't miss it. For younger children, you're able to hold up the family as a safe place. In less cohesive families, a system of true community offers a support network and assists the students in interpreting what's happening in and around their families. If you teach these kids how to fight for their families, maybe one day when they grow up and get married, they'll understand how to break the cycle in their own family relationships.

Is something designed once a year for parents, children, and small group leaders to build bridges and get acquainted with each other?

Do you cast vision with your small group leaders to help them understand practical ways they can partner with and encourage the family as a unit?

Is an expectation established for small group leaders for intentional personal connection with parents through email or a phone call several times a year?

Do small group leaders understand the value of encouraging high schoolers to fight for relationships with their parents?

GAUGE KEY

0	Not happening
20	Just getting started
40	Making some progress
60	Steadily moving
80	In high gear

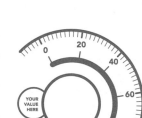

YOUR VALUE HERE

Elevate Community

C5

GRADUATED SYSTEM

Small group leaders are encouraged to graduate with the same kids and students into older age groups, especially in middle and high school.

When children are young, you can more easily change their leaders every year. A second grader can walk in, see an adult, and believe everything that big person says. And that second grader will tell the adult anything she's thinking, regardless of what her parents think. But when children move to middle school or high school, you have to earn that deep trust with them, and that takes time. And you probably won't have the time you need to create the kind of relationship teenagers will trust.

This is why it's so important to have small group leaders, especially for middle and high school students, remain involved with the same students for multiple years. As students go through life change and the stakes get higher, they need consistent voices in their lives, voices of people who will point them back to the principles they most need to hear. That can only happen if you have a graduated system, where leaders advance to the next grade along with the students they've been leading.

Everything changes when your leaders aren't approaching leadership like they're just babysitting a certain group for a year, but are investing in real relationships that will last a lifetime.

Do the leaders of your older kids make a multiple-year commitment to stay with their small groups?

Is a coleader model established so as a group grows, it can split if necessary and the kids/students will still have a familiar leader?

GAUGE KEY

0	Not happening
20	Just getting started
40	Making some progress
60	Steadily moving
80	In high gear

Everyone is connected to a caring leader and consistent group of peers

SPIRITUAL PRIORITIES

Small group leaders understand that part of their weekly responsibilities includes modeling and leading students in prayer, understanding Scripture, worship, and sharing their faith with others.

Again the goal of any ministry is to lead individuals to the place where they can lead themselves. One of the most powerful things that any leader can do is to model the key aspects of faith—especially those skills that will enable someone to continue to grow on their own. There are five faith skills every small group leader should consistently demonstrate for their kids. If every leader creatively practices these five skills in their group life each week it will provide an environment where kids and students can become self-feeders. Their spiritual growth really is connected to certain spiritual priorities in their life. It is important that every leader spends time every week shaping how they use and view Scripture, how they talk with God, and how they share their faith.

Are the small group leaders trained and comfortable with all five faith skills so they can model and help their kids and students grow in them?

Do the faith skills provide a consistent road map for implementing relevant, creative elements in each age group?

Can older students articulate the key disciplines of a growing faith?

GAUGE KEY

0	Not happening
20	Just getting started
40	Making some progress
60	Steadily moving
80	In high gear

Elevate Community

PERSONAL FAITH

When students graduate, they are aware of their spiritual identity and feel personally responsible to own their own faith.

There is really no concept of secondhand faith in Scripture. Ultimately everyone will be responsible for his or her own faith. Children naturally move toward independence as they head toward the college years. The older they get the more important it is for their faith to be identified as their own. Your goal is not to get kids or students to simply go to church, but to be the church. The worst thing a small group leader can do is to build a codependent relationship with a student; the most important thing a leader can do is to equip a student to champion his or her own personal faith. If we want students to be self-feeders, that means we have to continue to tweak their environments so they can ask hard questions, process and discuss complex issues, to think through "why" they believe what they believe so that it is actually something that will stick whenever they walk away.

Are kids and students increasingly looking up to their leaders for guidance in owning their own spiritual development?

Are the small group leaders aware of where every kid or student stands in their spiritual process and if they've each made a specific decision to become a Christian?

Does your church celebrate significant steps as a child or student makes faith more personal?

GAUGE KEY

0	Not happening
20	Just getting started
40	Making some progress
60	Steadily moving
80	In high gear

Everyone is connected to a caring leader and consistent group of peers

ACTIVITIES

MOVIE CLIP
MOVIE CLIP
MOVIE CLIP
MOVIE CLIP
MOVIE CLIP
MOVIE CLIP
MOVIE CLIP
MOVIE CLIP
MOVIE CLIP
MOVIE CLIP
MOVIE CLIP
MOVIE CLIP
MOVIE CLIP
MOVIE CLIP
MOVIE CLIP
MOVIE CLIP
MOVIE CLIP
MOVIE CLIP
MOVIE CLIP
MOVIE CLIP
MOVIE CLIP
MOVIE CLIP

In *Finding Forrester*, an unlikely mentorship develops between a mysterious old man who spies from a window and a young minority basketball player with a single mom, a C average, and exceptional test scores. The grumpy old man turns out to be a famous but recluse author—Forrester—who helps the young man, Jamal, find his voice at a critical point in his life. In one of the closing scenes, this is what the sixteen-year-old boy has to say about family.[4]

Losing family obliges us to find our family. Not always the family that is our blood but the family that can become our blood. And should we have the wisdom to open our door to this new family, we will find that the wishes we once had for the father who once guided us, for the brother who once inspired us ... The only thing left to say will be, "I wish I had seen this, or I wish I had done that, or I wish ..."

Later, Forrester wrote this about their friendship:
Someone I once knew wrote that we walk away from our dreams afraid that we may fail, or worse yet that we may succeed. While I knew so early that you would realize your dreams, I never imagined that I would once again realize my own. Seasons change, young man. And while I may have waited too long to see the things I've seen this past year, there is no doubt I would've waited too long had it not been for you.

We talk about the potential in second voices for all types and forms of family. What could happen in the lives of the adults or older teen-agers as they invest in the next generation?

We mentioned author Anne Lamott earlier in this chapter in a passage where she shared why she makes her son go to church. For more about her radical journey in faith and community, we recommend reading her book *Traveling Mercies*.

Similar in style, wit, and refreshing honesty, Donald Miller is well known for his book *Blue Like Jazz*, and he shares in *Think Orange* about a spiritual catalyst in his life. We thought it was worth repeating here.

"My father left when I was a toddler, and right about the time I was breaking into houses, a man at my church invited me to a morning book study and took me under his wing. He befriended me. His role was simple. He played catch with me, invited me over to eat with his family, and even gave me a shot at writing for a local newsletter. That one affirming voice in my life, I believe, kept me out of jail."

How many of the children or teenagers in your ministry have single parents? How many have divorced parents, so they come every other week or even less? When you plan special activities or talk to a large group, are you being sensitive to all family situations and universal needs (Father's and Mother's Day, for example)? A second voice is good for *everyone*, but critical for a few. Remember that you don't have to do it all by yourself. Ask around tactfully. Who else has a passion for this? There is potential in being intentional.

POST IT

As a warm-up at your next training, encourage staff and volunteers to write down a moment or person or experience that impacted or changed their lives spiritually. Give them a time limit. They can write more than one if they have extra time.

Then have them share at their tables or in small groups. This will help to build community and trust. After they've shared, challenge them to group these spiritual turning points into categories as best they can. Where is there overlap or similarities? What do they notice?

Have a spokesperson for each group summarize what the group talked about and then add their notes under the appropriate Spiritual Growth Catalyst (Life-changing Truth, Spiritual Disciplines, Personal Ministry, Significant Relationships, Pivotal Circumstances) on a board that you have ready in the front of the room. (Don't reveal the headings until this part of the activity.)

Lastly, talk about what you do on Sundays or during the week at church with families. Talk about ways you are already creating these kinds of opportunities. What areas could you emphasize more, and how? This is a great time to emphasize that small group relationships have the most potential to cut across all five areas. Demonstrate that visually as you share your commitment to providing community for everyone in the church. Ask for ideas on how you can better spread this vision to others who haven't heard it yet or who don't understand this philosophy. This creates a sense of team and ownership and helps you reach beyond this circle of influence to future generations.

ORANGE-OMETER

In these spaces, transfer your scores from the Component pages earlier in this chapter. Calculate your average score from the seven components and write it in the gauge below.

GAUGE KEY

0	Not happening
20	Just getting started
40	Making some progress
60	Steadily moving
80	In high gear

INTEGRATE STRATEGY

Synchronized Team	S1	
Designated Leader	S2	
Consistent Meetings	S3	
Common Language	S4	
Clear Wins	S5	
Strategic Programs	S6	
Systematic Training	S7	

REFINE THE MESSAGE

Strategic Teaching	M1	
Relevant Environments	M2	
Synchronized Content	M3	
Focused Truth	M4	
Engaging Presentation	M5	
Relational Experiences	M6	
Appealing Context	M7	

YOUR VALUE HERE

YOUR VALUE HERE

REACTIVATE THE FAMILY		ELEVATE COMMUNITY		LEVERAGE INFLUENCE	
Compelling Vision	F1	Church-Wide Focus	C1	Strategic Service	I1
Pro-Family Culture	F2	Invested Leaders	C2	Repeated Opportunities	I2
Parental Support	F3	Consistent Relationships	C3	Intentional Apprenticeship	I3
Family Experiences	F4	Family Reinforcement	C4	Targeted Studies	I4
Milestone Emphasis	F5	Graduated System	C5	Global Involvement	I5
Effective Family Time	F6	Spiritual Priorities	C6	Personalized Mission	I6
Community-Wide Focus	F7	Personal Faith	C7	Redemptive Purpose	I7

0   20   40   60   80
YOUR VALUE HERE

0   20   40   60   80
YOUR VALUE HERE

0   20   40   60   80
YOUR VALUE HERE

TWO
COMBINED
INFLUENCES MOBILIZE
GENERATIONS.

Leverage
Influence

Create consistent opportunities for students to
experience personal ministry

CHAPTER 8
LEVERAGE INFLUENCE

CREATE CONSISTENT OPPORTUNITIES FOR STUDENTS TO EXPERIENCE PERSONAL MINISTRY
Two combined influences mobilize generations

WHEN WE DON'T LEVERAGE INFLUENCE

Parents are programmed to see the church as a provider of services for their kids.

Leaders never recognize that the discipleship process is also about influencing a student to serve and care for others.

The church unintentionally fuels a self-centered and materialistic mindset in the hearts of kids.

Students establish a consumer mindset about the church.

Communities continue to perceive the church as institutional and insulated.

Individual families never experience a sense of calling and mission to make others a priority.

Kids/students fail to engage in one of the most critical experiences that contribute to their spiritual formation.

Students fail to experience and realize their calling to care for others, and they leave the church without a passion to pursue God's calling in their lives.

WHAT ELSE HAPPENS WHEN WE DON'T LEVERAGE INFLUENCE?

MOUNTAIN CLIMBING
How are you engaging students in service?

So what do you think would be more exciting: Going to classes that teach you about mountain climbing, or actually standing at the summit after a hard climb to get a firsthand look at the view? Imagine sitting in a classroom for several years and listening to someone describe the adventures related to climbing mountains. How would it affect you if you never climbed a mountain yourself? Do you think you would be more or less motivated to climb?

Here is a profound question: Do you think climbers climb just because they have heard about climbing, or because one day they started climbing?

Here are a few realities. If you never actually climb …

… you will miss the discovery of personal capacity.

… you will miss the passion of engaging with the mountain.

… you will miss the wonder that comes with seeing the view.

But this is more than just mountain climbing. The same principles hold true for kids and teenagers in the church. Somehow we believe that if we talk about the importance of faith and teach them how to show faith, they will automatically grow in faith. At what point do you think it is appropriate for students to grab some rope and start heading up the side of a mountain? When do you think a student should start doing ministry? Most churches spend a lot of energy trying to get students to come to programs where they talk about growing as Christians, but they forget that the way you grow is by experience.

Do you think service can be a catalyst for starting faith in someone's heart? Have you ever heard of or seen this happening? How can your church or ministry leverage service as an exciting starting place for nonbelievers?

NOTES

See if you agree with this: *Mountain climbers grow in their mountain climbing skills by climbing mountains.* Maybe the best way to help students grow in their faith is by orchestrating opportunities where they have to practically demonstrate or exercise what they believe. You have to make an intentional shift in the way you do ministry as a student transitions toward high school and into adulthood. In too many churches, students sit and listen instead of actually experiencing hands-on ministry.

If we really want students to be competent climbers, we need to start handing them some rope. We don't need to have them read another book about climbing; we need to take them up the mountain and help them experience it firsthand. Students need consistent opportunities to develop their faith, to see God show up in the triumphs and difficulties of ministry, and to experience how He wants them to influence others. If you give them enough rope to do that before they leave your church, maybe they will understand what it means to actually be the church wherever they go.

Make people feel significant by giving them something significant to do.

A couple of years ago at our Orange Conference, Donald Miller shared a story about a friend of his who was having problems with his daughter. The dad was worried because the daughter had gotten involved in a Goth lifestyle and was dating a guy who was bad news. As a frustrated dad, his technique for dealing with the situation was to yell at her and make her go to church. When he came to Don for advice, Don told him, "I think what your daughter is doing is choosing a better story."

He went on. "We're all designed to live inside a story. Your daughter was designed to play a role in a story. In the story she has chosen, there is risk, adventure, and pleasure. She is wanted and she is desired. In your story, she's yelled at, she feels guilty, and she feels unwanted. She's just choosing a story that is better than the one you're providing. Plus, in the midst of placing her in an awful story, you make her go to church. So you're associating a bad, boring story with God, who has a great story. Don't do that anymore. You have to tell a better story."

You can read more about how the dad stirred the hearts of his children toward action in *Think Orange* on page 207. Ultimately, his daughter and son became caught up in a real story with risk and adventure in which they were able to play the heroes. How are you painting a big picture and showing how the lives of preteens and teenagers in your ministry can play a part in God's better story?

How does the statement, "We're all designed to live inside a big story," make you feel? What role have you played in God's story up to this point? Do you think it's possible that the limited roles children and students are allowed to play (or even the roles they're excluded from because of their age) has something to do with their decreasing participation as they grow up in the church?

NOTES

The heart will gravitate toward whatever offers adventure and significance.

GIVE THEM AN ADVENTURE

One of the reasons some students walk away from the church is that they have found something more exciting to walk toward—they have discovered what seems to be a bigger story. When they look back at their church involvement, it was static and noneventful. They have never experienced the intoxicating kind of faith that comes when they allow God to work through their lives. They didn't have a direct encounter with ministry that gave them a personal sense of God's mission. They missed out on the passion that results when you collide with humanity to care for someone in a crisis situation.

> What *real* opportunities do you tap into in your local community and globally? Think about all the different experiences that teenagers encounter outside the church during this stage in life. Now compare that with what you have planned for them. Look around—what organizations can you partner with so they can have a firsthand, mind-blowing experience with a big God as they serve others?

NOTES

When your style of faith doesn't include anything dangerous or adventurous, you begin to drift toward other things that seem more interesting and meaningful. Be honest, what do average teenagers in the average church really experience? When do we stretch their faith? When do we push them into ministry situations where they have to depend on God to do something in them and through them? When do we consistently give them opportunities to develop a personal ministry? The average high school student can get a job, drive a car, apply to college, and open a bank account, but we rarely allow these same kids to lead or serve in ministry inside or outside of church.

What makes us think that students will do ministry when they leave us if they never do ministry while they are with us?

If what they have heard doesn't move from their heads to their hands, it will probably never make it to their hearts.

One of the best ways to stimulate faith is to give someone an opportunity to have a personal ministry.

At North Point we decided we were not going to create programming for teenagers on Sunday mornings. We weren't going to create any classes where they would sit and have Bible study. We decided we would focus on giving them opportunities to serve with us on Sunday morning. We wanted them to serve not simply because we needed their help, but because it would be critical to their spiritual growth.

Do you have competing systems at your church? In other words, is service a value, but people have to choose between that and community or worship? How can you simplify and reduce the number of choices and also plan strategically so more people can participate in and grow from what God is doing?

NOTES

You don't begin to serve when you feel compassion; you feel compassion as you begin to serve.

When we rethink the value of personal ministry, we move toward a more comprehensive model of discipleship.

Engaging a teenager in ministry is the best way to ensure …

A dynamic faith in God. (That's wonder.)

A personal identity in Christ. (That's discovery.)

A responsive heart toward others. (That's passion.)

If we don't encourage youth to serve,

Wonder fades.

Discovery is eclipsed.

Passion is extinguished.

When we rethink the value of personal ministry, we move toward an experiential and relational approach to curriculum.

Jesus did not teach the disciples to do ministry. He did ministry with the disciples while He taught them. Too often churches limit discipleship to a presentation-driven method. Many leaders, however, instinctively recognize that something more is required for spiritual formation. The goal is not to cover a body of information, but to engage young people in a process that results in life change.

Imagine you had six ninth-grade boys or girls for the next four years. What would you do to disciple them? You have no limitations and no distracting responsibilities. The sky's the limit. So what would you do together?

NOTES

I recently asked a group of seasoned leaders from around the country this same spiritual formation question. They each talked about different projects and mission endeavors. Some mentioned the amount of time they would devote to building the relationship. Some brought up authors they would want to read together. Toward the end of the conversation, we realized that no one had brought up taking them to any kind of classroom presentation.

Based on your own answers and theirs, what does this mean for us? Are we teaching students in a classroom for efficiency? Ideally, how could you bring the numbers down to smaller groups with consistent leaders and several years together? How can you free up their time to build deep relationships and serve together?

NOTES

When we rethink the value of personal ministry, we find a new way to measure ministry.

Senior leaders, parents, and student pastors have to be intentional about changing their priorities. They should rethink the pressure put on the average ministry to define success by the amount of programming or attendance. Instead of asking, "How many came last week?" they should ask, "What percentage of students are engaging in ministry?" or "What percentage of our resources and time is set aside for serving instead of being fed?"

As we're reconsidering how we measure success, let's take a closer look at the B-team. Many leaders focus on reaching A-team students who are popular or influential. But an untapped power of influence in a student ministry includes those students who are not so well-known. One could make the case that Jesus seemed to have a similar approach.

Jesus reached the world by leveraging the influence of common people and empowering them to do uncommon things.

Think through the teenagers you know and find out about ones you don't know as well. In your mind, pretend you are giving the popular, well-known student a hundred dollars' worth of attention. They are used to this, so it will seem like ten dollars to them. Take the same hundred dollars' worth of attention and give it to a student not in the mainstream, used to being on the sidelines, and it will feel like a thousand! Who is sitting on your sidelines with untapped potential? Ask around.

NOTES

For a great sports illustration of this B-team concept to use in training, read page 215 in *Think Orange* about Texas Tech football player Matt Williams.

PROGRAMMED TO OVERPROTECT

Going back to our earlier example, it may be terrifying as parents and leaders to think of our sons or daughters mountain climbing. We might be tempted to take a reactionary approach that prevents them from the potentially dangerous and risky business of mountain climbing, at least until they are older. But this really means that we care more about their safety than their faith. We would sacrifice the things they could learn and experience just to protect them from the possibility of getting hurt. Parenting this way demands the question, "What happens one day when they are on their own?"

They were meant to be part of an adventurous story. This is a mission that requires us to engage with culture in order to rescue a generation of hurting and disconnected people. In some ways, it would be better for our sons and daughters to get hurt and learn lessons while they are still with us than to launch out on their own without any experience in climbing. Or even worse: If they never learn to climb while they are with you, they may never try at all. Then what happens to their passion? What happens to their hearts? What if they were made for something more?

As leaders and parents, our primary calling is not to keep our children in the church, but to lead them to be the church.

Do you know any stories about children and students and families being on mission together to help broken people and tell them about our big God? How do you collect these stories? How can you use them to celebrate, inspire, and encourage small group leaders and other families?

NOTES

For an inspiring email about a sixth-grade boy whose life was changed by the opportunity to be part of God's bigger story, read pages 218–219 in *Think Orange*.

When we help children and students leverage their influence, we give them the weapons they need to rescue a generation. In doing so, we influence the next generation to participate in the call of David:

"Tell the next generation the praiseworthy deeds of the LORD, his power, and the wonders he has done ... so the next generation would know them, even the children yet to be born, and they in turn would tell their children. Then they would put their trust in God."[1]

The greatest calling of the church and the home is to lead our sons and daughters into a growing relationship with Jesus Christ.

The best gift we can ever give them is to enable them to play an active role in His story of restoration and redemption.

INFLUENCE

THE SEVEN COMPONENTS TO LEVERAGE INFLUENCE

CREATE CONSISTENT OPPORTUNITIES FOR STUDENTS TO EXPERIENCE PERSONAL MINISTRY

We will stand in front of teenagers week after week and tell them, "You're significant and God has a plan for your life. You're significant and God wants to *do* something with your life. You're significant, significant, significant." But until we give them something significant to do as teenagers, they won't understand what their significance really means. That's why we need to lead them in leveraging their influence, for their own good and for the good of the world around them. If you're doing that, you'll see components like these in your ministry.

These seven components will help clarify what it can look like when a church is becoming Orange. Use them as points of reference to gauge how well you are doing in each area.

I1. STRATEGIC SERVICE

I2. REPEATED OPPORTUNITIES

I3. INTENTIONAL APPRENTICESHIP

I4. TARGETED STUDIES

I5. GLOBAL INVOLVEMENT

I6. PERSONALIZED MISSION

I7. REDEMPTIVE PURPOSE

Leverage Influence

11 STRATEGIC SERVICE

Leaders and parents embrace service as an essential part of the discipleship process.

Plugging students into service is one of the greatest things you can do in the window of time you have with teenagers. Training, preparation, vision-casting, and mentoring are essential at this stage, not just for the task at hand but for the broader concept of service. This is personal discipleship, so the service options should be as involved and as demanding as appropriate for the individual student. You don't disciple them by simply getting them to worship and pray; you disciple them by plugging them in to do work and ministry so they can experience what God wants to do through them.

How is service linked to discipleship?

How do you celebrate and recognize those who are getting involved in ministry?

Do you know the percentage of students plugged in and serving?

(NOTE: Ask this question as a way to evaluate your ministry, rather than asking how many are attending.)

GAUGE KEY

0	Not happening
20	Just getting started
40	Making some progress
60	Steadily moving
80	In high gear

Create consistent opportunities for students to experience personal ministry

REPEATED OPPORTUNITIES

Age-group directors and family ministry team members implement and monitor a systematic plan to help kids and students plug in to specific ministries inside the church.

If teenagers don't have an opportunity to serve from ninth through twelfth grades, they may walk away from your church never experiencing what God wants to do through them. The chances are also good that they'll walk out of your church and think it didn't mean a whole lot. It may have been a good experience for a time, but is it relevant to real life? You can teach students and teenagers that they are significant to God, but until you give them something significant to do, they're not going to truly embrace their significance in God's bigger story.

Does your organization make it simple for students and children to get involved at different levels and ages in something significant, like leading a small group or greeting in a hallway or large group room?

Are there consistent opportunities to systematically serve over a period of months, not just occasionally or once a year?

What are you doing as kids move to third and fourth grade and then middle school to raise this value and give them even more opportunities to plug in?

GAUGE KEY

0	Not happening
20	Just getting started
40	Making some progress
60	Steadily moving
80	In high gear

Leverage Influence

INTENTIONAL APPRENTICESHIP

Adult volunteers are trained and encouraged to apprentice kids and students in various areas of ministry.

Leaders in the church should engage teenagers in every ministry department and service area. Set these students free to do a thousand different ministries, and attach them to other adults like volunteer captains and coaches. The more adult influences you can put in their lives, the more you're building a foundation for their future involvement.

Each of these leaders needs to be sold out to the idea that this four-year window with a high school student is the formative time in that young person's life. The role they have in guiding and apprenticing these students is one of the most important missions they'll ever have. The training can't be haphazard. The responsibilities can't be random. Adult leaders, no matter what the ministry, should take seriously the process of showing these students how their service makes a lasting and important impact.

When and where are adult volunteers trained in mentoring and investing in teenagers to help them develop their gifts?

Can adult leaders and their apprentices participate in training times together, in a format that enhances the experience and effectiveness of both?

Do leaders see their relationships with teenagers as equally important for discipleship as they do their other responsibilities in small groups?

GAUGE KEY

0	Not happening
20	Just getting started
40	Making some progress
60	Steadily moving
80	In high gear

Create consistent opportunities for students to experience personal ministry

14

TARGETED STUDIES
Specific series and curriculums are designed as catalysts to mobilize students to do ministry.

Incite the passion of students by doing a group study at least once a year that dives into our need to serve. Setting aside time to do a Bible study series on this issue for kids or students raises it as a value. By attaching biblical imperatives to their practical ministry actions, students will be able to distinguish between a nice humanitarian social activity and the powerful and compelling call of God to care for others. It's essential they understand the difference between the work of man and the work of God.

Part of this understanding is as foundational as why God put us on the planet: We don't ask students to serve because God's work won't get done without them, but because He's created them to grow through service. Students don't need to serve because the church needs it. Instead, students need to serve because they won't grow as Christians if they don't serve. This is part of God's plan to grow and develop a believer's faith.

Will there be a series at least once a year mobilizing students to serve?

How do you communicate the biblical principles involved in service?

Are parents clued in to the fact that this is a value in your ministry?

Do students understand the difference between just doing good deeds and being an active part of God's bigger story?

What tools have you given parents to help reinforce to their students that we don't just go to church; we are the church?

GAUGE KEY

0	Not happening
20	Just getting started
40	Making some progress
60	Steadily moving
80	In high gear

Leverage Influence

15 GLOBAL INVOLVEMENT

Student and children's teams create consistent opportunities for small groups and families to serve the community outside the church (locally and globally).

Don't make it just about your church—give students a bigger picture, a bigger mission, and a bigger adventure so they can understand the part they play in the bigger story. Cross the street or cross the continents, but build a broader perspective of God's global presence into your young people. Imagine the impact when, as adults, they reflect on their time as teens and think, "My church showed me the world."

When these global experiences can happen for your students (and on an appropriate scale, children), they'll be transformed. The kids who get off the airplane won't be the same kids who got on the airplane. When possible, take your team as a group so everyone can share a common experience and common memories. They'll help each other remember the power of what they did and saw, and they'll interpret a new future for one another as they frame a new perspective of what God can do through them.

Are there opportunities for families to serve together and do local projects with their small groups?

What kinds of international mission projects are encouraged?

How many mission trips do you host where teens and kids can serve with their parents?

Are there projects families can support together, like child sponsorship programs or purposeful times of prayer for a specific people or ministry?

Is your church characterized more by educating or experiencing?

GAUGE KEY

0	Not happening
20	Just getting started
40	Making some progress
60	Steadily moving
80	In high gear

Create consistent opportunities for students to experience personal ministry

16 PERSONALIZED MISSION

Events, programs, and small group environments are leveraged to celebrate and challenge how kids and students use their gifts in personal ministry.

We're trying to help teenagers understand that they're not called to *go* to church; they're called to *be* the church. Within that challenge exists an opportunity for students to maximize their developing personalities, their passionate interests, their academic learning, even their likes and dislikes. These are the years in which students are discovering how God has gifted them for every aspect of life. How ironic that the church is one of the least likely places they get to exercise those gifts.

Do your small group leaders monitor how and where kids and students are plugging in? Do they encourage students to get involved?

How do students connect what they can do with what the church needs?

Who helps students apply what they're learning in school and extracurricular activities to increase their influence and impact?

Do small group leaders in later high school years stay in contact with their students through their first year in college to help them navigate life and make good decisions?

GAUGE KEY

0	Not happening
20	Just getting started
40	Making some progress
60	Steadily moving
80	In high gear

YOUR VALUE HERE

Leverage Influence

REDEMPTIVE PURPOSE

Students and children understand their place in a bigger story and anticipate opportunities to communicate that story to others.

Do students feel like they're a part of telling God's story to a broken world? When you turn the wonder, discovery, and passion dials, they should experience Jesus in such a dynamic way that they may walk away from your church into the next phase of life, but they can never get over what happened with God. When they are passionate about giving their lives to the world rather than being self-absorbed, they realize they're created for something much, much bigger than themselves. Your measure shouldn't be how many students are coming to your programs, but how many students are realizing their redemptive purpose and living that out in their lives.

Do all the preteens and teenagers understand that everything comes back to their belief in Christ?

How do students and children connect embracing God's story with the service opportunities provided?

What options are available to allow a student to reflect after a few years of college to see if the gospel-service connection is still intact?

GAUGE KEY

0	Not happening
20	Just getting started
40	Making some progress
60	Steadily moving
80	In high gear

Create consistent opportunities for students to experience personal ministry

ACTIVITIES

Can you think of a time when someone got you really excited about a new opportunity? You were looking forward to it, maybe even went to a class to get ready, but for whatever reason, you never had a chance to experience it? Or maybe you had a life-changing, hands-on experience and came back to find you were still expected to just sit and listen. Or maybe you had a great idea for a way to help others but you weren't taken seriously.

HOW DID YOU RESPOND?

FIRSTHAND

TAKE A POLL

DOES YOUR CHURCH SEE SERVICE AS A LEGITIMATE WAY TO GROW SPIRITUALLY?

IS IT IN YOUR MISSION STATEMENT OR ON A WALL, BUT NOT ACTUALLY HAPPENING CONSISTENTLY?

ARE OPPORTUNITIES OPEN TO EVERYONE, OR DOES IT FEEL LIKE SOMETHING ONLY A FEW INSIDERS KNOW ABOUT?

If you're not sure, take an informal poll.

SIDELINED
OR IN THE GAME

If you look at all your programming, events, and mission/service opportunities, are your children and students more often spectators or participants?

If you had to put it into a ratio of engaged versus watching, what would it be?

What's one element you can modify to get them out of their seats and into the action?

Who has a heart for plugging children and students into ministry that could lead this?

Get someone in your mind and plan to get together with that person soon to talk about this chapter.

MOVIE CLIP!

The movie Pay It Forward shows that sometimes the simplest idea can make the biggest difference. In this drama, a teacher gives a special assignment that one boy takes very seriously.[2]

TREVOR MCKENNEY: SO YOU'LL, LIKE, FLUNK US IF WE DON'T CHANGE THE WORLD?

EUGENE: WELL, NO, I WOULDN'T DO THAT. BUT YOU MIGHT JUST SQUEAK BY WITH A C.

So Trevor comes up with a simple plan with potentially big dividends and draws it on the board for his class. He plans to help three people and then ask them to pay it forward for three more people instead of paying him back so that it starts a chain reaction.

But there were some setbacks and frustrations along the way.

TREVOR: I GUESS IT'S HARD FOR PEOPLE WHO ARE SO USED TO THINGS THE WAY THEY ARE— EVEN IF THEY'RE BAD—TO CHANGE. 'CAUSE THEY KIND OF GIVE UP. AND WHEN THEY DO, EVERYBODY KIND OF LOSES.

Is it possible for one idea to change the world? Watch the whole movie to find out. But believing in the potential of each person can make a difference.

What ideas could you help unleash in the children, teenagers, and families in your church and ministry? We can't wait to hear the stories!

ORANGE-OMETER

In these spaces, transfer your scores from the component pages earlier in this chapter. Calculate your average score from the seven components and write it in the gauge below.

GAUGE KEY

0	Not happening
20	Just getting started
40	Making some progress
60	Steadily moving
80	In high gear

INTEGRATE STRATEGY

Synchronized Team **S1**

Designated Leader **S2**

Consistent Meetings **S3**

Common Language **S4**

Clear Wins **S5**

Strategic Programs **S6**

Systematic Training **S7**

YOUR VALUE HERE

REFINE THE MESSAGE

Strategic Teaching **M1**

Relevant Environments **M2**

Synchronized Content **M3**

Focused Truth **M4**

Engaging Presentation **M5**

Relational Experiences **M6**

Appealing Context **M7**

YOUR VALUE HERE

REACTIVATE THE FAMILY		ELEVATE COMMUNITY		LEVERAGE INFLUENCE	
Compelling Vision	F1	Church-Wide Focus	C1	Strategic Service	I1
Pro-Family Culture	F2	Invested Leaders	C2	Repeated Opportunities	I2
Parental Support	F3	Consistent Relationships	C3	Intentional Apprenticeship	I3
Family Experiences	F4	Family Reinforcement	C4	Targeted Studies	I4
Milestone Emphasis	F5	Graduated System	C5	Global Involvement	I5
Effective Family Time	F6	Spiritual Priorities	C6	Personalized Mission	I6
Community-Wide Focus	F7	Personal Faith	C7	Redemptive Purpose	I7

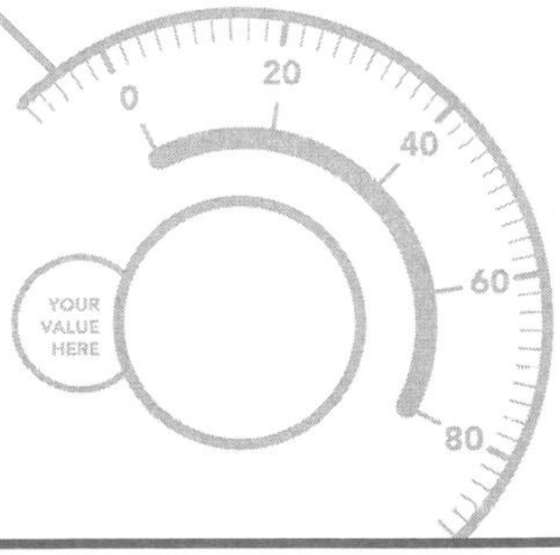

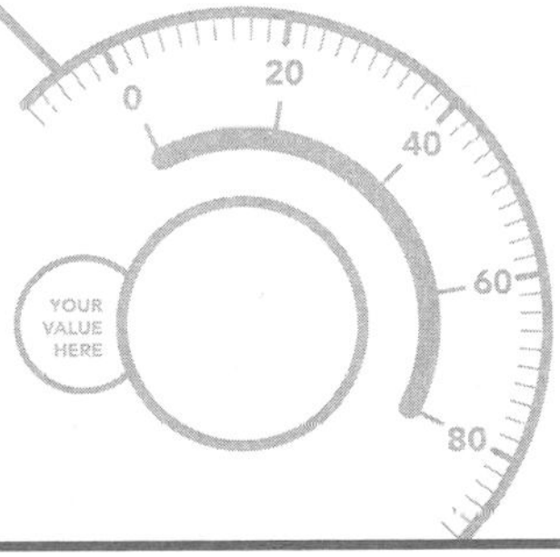

0 20 40 60 80
YOUR VALUE HERE

0 20 40 60 80
YOUR VALUE HERE

0 20 40 60 80
YOUR VALUE HERE

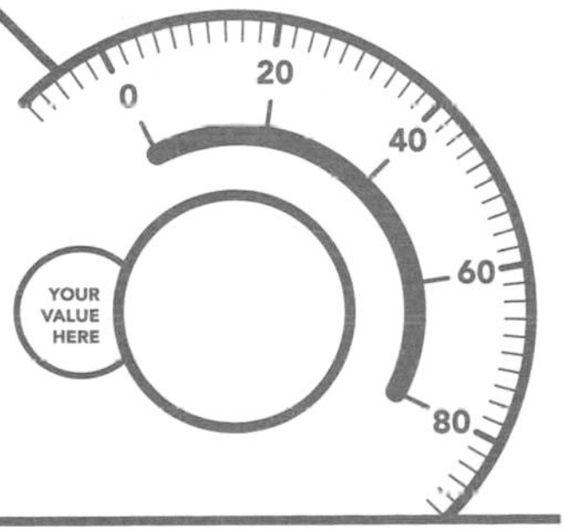

YOU CAN'T GET
ON THE SAME
PAGE
IF YOU DON'T GET
IN THE SAME
ROOM.

CHAPTER 9

Conclusion

ALIGNMENT

CONCLUSION

ALIGNMENT

In 1995 I was getting ready to change jobs to start North Point Community Church with Andy and five others. I needed to switch all of my information to a new computer. The thing I loved about the Mac was that it smiled at you when you booted it up every morning. It was a warm, friendly, Christian kind of thing. But this time something different happened: I booted it up and my computer frowned. In those days, if a Macintosh frowned at you, it meant there was a major problem. The thing was that I had not backed up seven or eight *years'* worth of messages, information, finances, photos.

If you've ever gone through this, it's like watching your house burn down. I remember picking up my dead computer and taking it to the computer store. Frantic, I put it down on the desk and said, "I don't care what you do, but you've got to save my information. I don't want to lose my information." They started tinkering with it and trying to figure out what was wrong and I asked them if I could stay and watch. I could tell they weren't sure why anyone would want to do that, but I just wanted to be close to it. It's like taking your child to the hospital.

So I'm sitting there praying to God, knowing there was so much here that I wanted to save. The guys looked at it for a few hours and then they said they were going to get lunch. I said, "Wait a minute, you can't leave until this is resolved." They said they'd be back in thirty minutes, so I asked if I could just stay there. They agreed.

So they left for lunch, and it was traumatic for me. I was sitting there with my computer and I was looking at it and praying and promising God all kinds of promises if He'd just give me my information back … then all of the sudden, I had this impulse to push the button to release the CD-ROM drive. When I hit the button, a drawer popped out and I saw what was inside it. I knew immediately what had happened. I'd seen my four-year-old daughter walking around the house playing with things. She'd picked up a CD that actually had an old system on it. She put it in the drawer, like she'd seen me do so many times, and closed it.

When the technicians got back and I showed it to them, they explained it to me like this: "Here's what your computer was doing. When you hit the electric impulse or power button to get it to start, it began to look for the information it needed so it would know how to behave. And as it went looking to see what it was supposed to do, it saw some information from the old system screaming at it, saying 'Here we are, we know what to do, just follow our instructions.' And it would go over there and get a little bit of the old information, but then it would hear the new system that existed in the machine calling, 'No, no, no … come over here. We'll tell you what to do.' So it would jump back and forth between the old and the new until it literally had a mental breakdown. It's what technicians call a 'systems conflict.'" Once the old information was removed, the new system was able to function as it should.

Can you remember your first computer? What kind was it, and what did you use it for (school, work, games)? Think about a time that your technology failed you in a major way. What happened? How did you feel and what did you do to resolve the issue?

NOTES

off multiple systems or two systems that are entirely different. An old system is driving thought and a new system is driving thought. One of your jobs as a leader is to gather your team around the table so you can modify your systems together. *Effective organizations create a culture that is intentional about rethinking and upgrading their systems.*

How many systems are driving your ministry or team right now? What words would you use to describe your systems? Do your systems tend to be simple or complex, more organic or more structured? Is your staff or team split, with some preferring old systems and some trying to create new ones? What is the result of this systems conflict in your world?

NOTES

You see, the problem in churches is rarely the lack of a system. Every church has some type of invisible code that drives its decisions and values. But conflict happens when everyone is not operating off the same system. It is an issue of alignment. One of the most important things that any team can do is become intentional about upgrading together and working off the same system. You never have to work at becoming misaligned, but you have to work consistently at staying on the same page. Some of you are frustrated right now and here's part of the reason why: You're working

There are a few key questions you should regularly ask your team to see if you're upgrading systems in the way that you should.

What kind of meetings do you have?

I'm not asking if you're having meetings, because I'm sure that you are. People ask me all the time about the key to what happened at North Point. Please hear me on this: I absolutely think there was a God-thing that happened with the six of us who started it. But the key was not that we started with a blank page, because I know a lot of churches that start with a blank page, then they fizzle and fade. The key is that from the very beginning we met on a regular basis to stay on the same page. Every Monday morning for two hours, for at least ten years, we met and read books together and learned and wrestled and debated—we debated all the *hows* because we already agreed on the whys.

Because we agreed on the core, transcendent truths that made up our DNA, we were free to tweak our systems all day long. So sometimes we debated, argued, fought, even got in each other's faces about things—and that's okay. It doesn't cost you relationally as long as you will not compromise on what is timeless and what you're trying to highlight. This is an important part of the process because, as you grow, there is a tendency to back away from these principles and the way you govern and work together. And over time, you'll slip into this management style of people not having input and ownership.

Let's be honest. It's easier to have a management style that doesn't allow for team input and ownership. But it breeds institutionalism. So instead of an organic group of engaged people working together toward a common goal, you will reduce your staff to paid employees who simply maintain your decisions. It happens and it can even happen subtly. There's always a drift toward too much control. Systems are not meant to control—

they are meant to serve. So if you really do value team, there needs to be a certain kind of meeting to breed the culture you want.

Quickly make a list of the meetings you've led or attended in the last few days or weeks. What management style did you and other leaders use? How engaged did people in the room feel? How free were they to disagree? Do you and others look forward to meetings or dread them? What would make you want to not just attend but actively participate?

NOTES

FAMILY MINISTRY THREADS

It is critical for those who lead various age groups to meet consistently. Certain issues tie a family ministry team together. These threads establish a kind of code that should be the basis for meeting agendas and interdependent relationships. When people ask why it is important for the family ministry team to meet frequently, this list shows why. Age-group leaders can attempt to approach these issues independently, or they can collectively decide they will be more effective if they are responsible for them together.

These are topics the team should discuss, debate, and decide together, and they should be rethought and revisited in some way at every meeting. They will help determine how effectively the team is driving toward the mission of combining the influences of churches and families to impact the next generation.

We've arranged sample questions according to the five Essentials as a suggested guide to generate discussion for your team meetings. Use them or add your own and start meeting.

STRATEGY

THE LEARNING THREAD

It is important for key age-group leaders or directors to adopt a continual learning approach to ministry. The accountability that can happen within a family ministry team allows them to become better specialists in their age groups and to develop as generalists to oversee all ministries.

What books are we reading as a team?

What off-site meetings have we planned as a team?

What responsibilities are we assigning team members outside of their regular tasks to help them expand their knowledge base?

What learning environments/conferences will we attend together?

THE TRANSITION THREAD

Churches traditionally look at transition between grades as something that happens on promotion Sunday at the beginning of a new school year. Instead, the transition should be planned creatively months before it happens, and leaders may cross over into other areas to help manage the communication and changes smoothly.

What kind of orientation do we have for parents, kids, and students transitioning into...
... preschool?
... elementary?
... middle school?
... high school?
... college?

What printed/electronic materials have we established that help families understand how all the age-group ministries work together?

How is the calendar synchronized to promote students at strategic times?

MESSAGE
THE PRODUCTION THREAD
The learning curve accelerates when team members share resources and discoveries related to technology, video, programming, and other elements. Occasional collective planning can stimulate creativity and provide a great venue to evaluate the relevance of each other's ministry.

What new tools are we using to capture the imagination?

What musical, drama, or technical talent can we share to help each other's ministries?

What about equipment? Are there new technologies we can share?

How are we rotating to evaluate each other's environments and give input?

THE CONTENT THREAD
The goal of a family ministry team is to establish a comprehensive plan that builds content, consistent relationships, and core experiences into the lives of kids and teenagers. The team has to consistently evaluate and monitor the quality of the environments designed to communicate principles and provide meaningful experiences.

What experiences can we create that enhance the content?

Who are some volunteers/leaders we can coach to be great communicators?

How can we make sure every leader and parent understands the master plan?

What kind of promotions and decorations are we using to enhance the weekly content or monthly themes?

FAMILY
THE PARENT THREAD
Parents are not seen as sidelined supporters of the ministry but as partners. Since most moms and dads parent children of multiple ages, church leaders should strive to break down the silos and create interconnectivity. As a team, leaders constantly clarify a unified plan that cuts across all departments to protect the family and programming from competing systems.

How does a parent connect with the information they need from our church?

What consistent resources are going home, and are they being used?

Are there parent focus groups we can establish to give us input?

Who are the influential parents who can champion the partnerships to other parents?

What small group studies or materials can we use to cast vision to parents?

COMMUNITY
THE GROUP THREAD
Age-group leaders believe a small group context is the best possible environment for life-change. Across all ministries, they resist a classroom mindset and establish a graduating system that features a relationship with the small group leader as pivotal. The team works to develop an organization driven by community.

What is the ratio of leaders to kids and students in our groups?

What are we doing to raise the value of community for every age group?

What events are we hosting to raise the level of participation?

Do we have clearly defined, measurable goals for groups?

Are we getting unsolicited feedback from kids/teenagers who say they are enjoying their group experience?

INFLUENCE
THE VOLUNTEER THREAD

A cohesive message to volunteers about how they fit into the big picture of spiritual growth for a child is essential. If staff doesn't work closely together, volunteers will feel disconnected as well. A meeting to clarify a master plan for training and developing volunteers keeps everyone on the same page.

Are we creating regular and varied opportunities for teenagers to serve?

What percentage of the students are plugging in to ministry?

What can we do to make sure all adult ministry team leaders are apprenticing students?

How are we getting families and teenagers involved in local and global efforts?

When the family ministry team meets together on a consistent basis, the team:

values the interdependent relationships that are critical to success

draws lines between healthy competition and unhealthy competition

makes collective learning and input a priority provides a platform for the unfiltered debate that is necessary to improve systems

allows focus of resources to make a more powerful impact

Where are your primary sources of learning?

We should all be learning from the Bible, and we know that. So I'm going to give you permission to learn from someone who is not a Bible scholar. To say that it's okay to learn from something in the community or to learn from culture. It's even okay to learn from corporations.

A guy sent me a Facebook message the other day asking, "Don't you think the church is becoming too corporate?"

I responded, "Well yeah, I think that's possible. You can take corporate rules and they just won't fit your situation. So you'll need to filter and see what is applicable." But honestly, most churches I meet aren't corporate enough. The genius of people from corporations and other places is still from God, created by God. God gave them their ingenuity and ability to think that way. Before you take a shot at someone and say you won't listen to him because he's an outsider, you need to apply that same logic.

We can learn powerful things from outsiders. As long as you have to manage people, build facilities, watch your budget, orchestrate programs, and reach goals, you can learn a lot from the corporate world. I don't believe everything I hear out there, but I don't believe everything I hear from preachers, either. I'm going to take your theology through a filter, too. We should learn from anything and everything we can.

I came across a great example of this in the *Harvard Business Review* in an article about Pixar. I want to share these operating principles because when it comes to our own organizations, I think we can learn a lot.

1 **Everyone must have the freedom to communicate with anyone.** Every director or assistant or part-time staff member should have permission to speak freely with any high-level leader. If you have to, create times each week or each month specifically for free communication.

2 **It must be safe for everyone to share or offer their ideas.** One of my staff members actually said, "I think it's the opposite of this in most churches."

3 **We must stay close to innovations happening in the academic community.** There's a lot happening in the greater community that we should learn from, both in seminaries and colleges and from some other great people in the country trying to understand how to make our systems better.[1]

How do you routinely simplify your organization?

One of the things that stops the momentum or slows your organization down is complexity. You've piled and piled more stuff on, and you wake up one day and it's not moving the way it should anymore. So we need to create "stop-doing lists." The best way to start moving again is to drop some stuff. There are some things in your organization that take your energy away, and you've got enough sense to know what they are.

If we know it's going to cost us, are we really willing to pay the price to simplify? You see, it doesn't take leadership to kill something that's not working. It takes leadership to kill something that is working, so something else can work better. If you kill something that's not working, no one gets mad. But if you kill something that is working, you've got a whole bunch of people upset. You have to develop a pattern in your organization of being able to make hard decisions and to make some hard calls so something else can work better. Otherwise you won't have the kind of energy wrapped around your team that's necessary for moving you past the barrier you're facing.

Have you ever noticed that you don't have to work at getting complicated or complex; you have to work at staying simple? The gravitational pull is always toward complexity, never toward simplicity. And complexity can be the enemy of momentum and change. The simple model has a better chance to gain momentum because it is focused. Do you have a system where you are constantly pruning things out? To come up with your "stop-doing list," ask if the programs you're leading match your purpose. You can't change when you are overloaded because you can't turn fast enough.

Some things are worth repeating. If you haven't made a stop-doing list yet, go back to page 53. You might also have thought of more things to include that are draining more than they're adding. Don't forget to put deadlines for when this change needs to happen and to think about who you need to communicate this change to first so they don't hear about it from someone else.

What needs to change radically in your ministry?

You need to have the conversation in a number of different ways. Invite new staff members to tell you what they think needs to change before they are too used to the way things are. Ask younger leaders what they would change if they were in charge. If there is insecurity in your leadership or team that keeps you from pursuing change, you run the danger of becoming outdated and irrelevant. And when you make a change, really change. Don't go halfway and stop. Some churches never make the impact they should because they don't follow through with change. There's this myth that if we make changes slowly enough, we can sneak them in and no one will notice. Here's a profound thought: If you are hoping to make change so gradually that no one notices, then chances are no one will really notice. Sometimes it's the abrupt and radical change that sends you in a new direction and gets everyone's attention.

Change is important because it's critical to your MISSION.

When you change something radically it reminds everyone that the only thing sacred is the mission. It reminds your congregation, your volunteers, and everyone in your organization that this model is temporary. Every time you work at creating a culture of change, you are prompting people to remember your mission. Whenever you create a culture where things don't change, people think the model is the mission. But we have to draw a line of distinction between the two, or people think the program must be our mission because it hasn't changed in ten or twenty years.

When you change something on the inside of your organization, people begin to see you're serious about reaching the people on the outside. Our mission is to do what Jesus said to do before He left the planet—to make disciples. It's very important for people on the inside to see that they are not the priority, but that the people on the outside are. And if you're so afraid of the people on the inside that you're not willing to reach those on the outside, you are afraid of the wrong thing. You're afraid of who you're trying to keep, and you need to trade fears. Radical change sends a very clear message that this isn't about us; this is about them.

Change is important because it's critical to your REPUTATION.

I don't know if you're aware of it, but the church in America (it really doesn't matter the denomination) has a bad image right now. In other words, there's a certain perception by the people outside the church and that's why they're not coming to church. People outside the church will start believing that you really care about them and that you have a passion for them when you're willing to change for their sake, for their families and their communities. It's time to convince them that we are not fighting against them, but for them.

It will also change their perception of what you think about them. I think our biggest problem is what *they* think we think about them. I don't think they're disinterested in our teaching or our programs. They just don't believe we have their best interests in mind or that we really care about them. But imagine what it would be like if we could say, "We built this, we're doing this for *you*!" The reason we need to get involved in family ministries in our communities is not simply because it's a great way to evangelize. If the church doesn't roll up its sleeves and help marriages win and help parents win and help families win, then who will? The church has the best opportunity to do that. What can you radically change that sends a message to the outside that they are a priority for you?

Change is important because it's critical to your FAITH.

I want you to walk away with this: When you change something radically, it demonstrates what it means to trust God with *your* life and ministry. It's been a while since some of us were really out on a limb trusting God to show up. When was the last time you made such a radical change that you had to completely depend on God? We're the biggest hypocrites in the world when we won't change what we need to because of fear, but we still expect people outside the church to trust a God they don't even know with their whole lives.

Something powerful happens when leaders get on the same page and push to innovate and discover more effective ways to influence the community.

Some of you are leaders in your twenties. Here's a question: If you were in charge, what would you change about the ministry where you are involved?

JOURNAL

Learn to sit at the table with a respectful attitude and challenge the process. Remember it's your generation that is at stake if the right changes never happen in the church.

What about those of you in your thirties and forties? What should you change now? Are you working from memory and not your imagination?

JOURNAL

Many of you are in critical positions of leadership. You

are the bridge between new ideas and established traditions. Why don't you decide to walk out the door and walk back in as the new leader to embrace changes? For a moment in time you have some authority, and what you do in the next five to ten years will determine the future of the church.

Then there are those of you in your fifties and sixties. You have paid some costly dues to lead the church so far. Some of you have large amounts of relational change in your pockets with people who have been in church for years. Maybe it's time to spend the change.

You can either drift into retirement and not make waves, or you can leverage your influence to pave the way for things to change. What will it be? Your greatest legacy may not be what you hand off to the next leader, but how you hand it off.

WHAT IF

What if every age leader in your ministry decided to pursue creating a culture of change?

What if you rallied volunteers and parents to rethink how they partner for the next generation?

What if you started having dangerous conversations, every week or month, about what needs to improve or be redesigned in your ministry?

If you want to get on the same page, you have to get in the same room consistently.

Please don't stop meeting.

Please keep rethinking everything.
Please implement the kinds of changes that will capture the imagination of the next generation, so they will be amazed at what God wants to do in your church.

At the end of this manual we've created and attached a few tools we hope you will find helpful, like an Agenda Template for your team meetings and Planning Sheets to work on individual components.

GO UP—celebrate your reading of this manual with the families of people on your team or in your ministry by watching the movie *Up* together.[2] Have everyone sign up to bring something to share, or even trade picnic-basket-type meals. Spread out in a common area on blankets. There are many fun ways to use this amazing film to jump-start conversations about families, relationships, and multiple generations, our dreams, and our desires for adventure—and how we can miss out when we get stuck in the past. Share with them what you've discovered in this process and sketch out a plan of needed tweaks and changes. Get in the habit of celebrating progress, sharing your vision for the future, and asking people to join you in making it come true.

Then start the process all over again.

THE SKY'S THE LIMIT!

Appendix

ORANGE-OMETER

In these spaces, transfer your scores from the component pages. Calculate your average score from the seven components and write it in the gauge below.

GAUGE KEY

0	Not happening
20	Just getting started
40	Making some progress
60	Steadily moving
80	In high gear

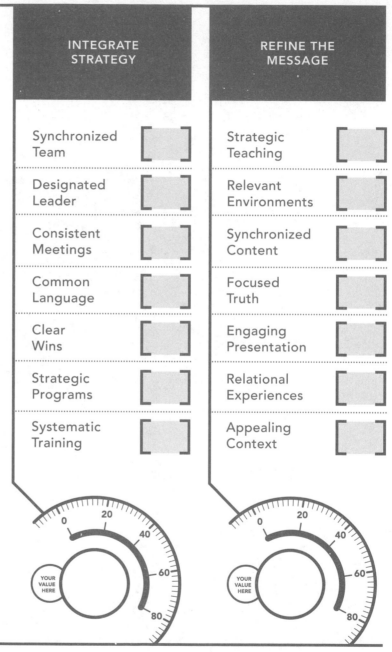

INTEGRATE STRATEGY

- Synchronized Team
- Designated Leader
- Consistent Meetings
- Common Language
- Clear Wins
- Strategic Programs
- Systematic Training

REFINE THE MESSAGE

- Strategic Teaching
- Relevant Environments
- Synchronized Content
- Focused Truth
- Engaging Presentation
- Relational Experiences
- Appealing Context

REACTIVATE THE FAMILY	ELEVATE COMMUNITY	LEVERAGE INFLUENCE
Compelling Vision	Church-Wide Focus	Strategic Service
Pro-Family Culture	Invested Leaders	Repeated Opportunities
Parental Support	Consistent Relationships	Intentional Apprenticeship
Family Experiences	Family Reinforcement	Targeted Studies
Milestone Emphasis	Graduated System	Global Involvement
Effective Family Time	Spiritual Priorities	Personalized Mission
Community-Wide Focus	Personal Faith	Redemptive Purpose

YOUR VALUE HERE

0   20   40   60   80

YOUR VALUE HERE

0   20   40   60   80

YOUR VALUE HERE

0   20   40   60   80

ORANGE-OMETER

If you prefer, write in your own terms for the components that more closely correspond to your ministry's language. Evaluate your score in each area and calculate the average, writing it in the gauge below.

GAUGE KEY

0	Not happening
20	Just getting started
40	Making some progress
60	Steadily moving
80	In high gear

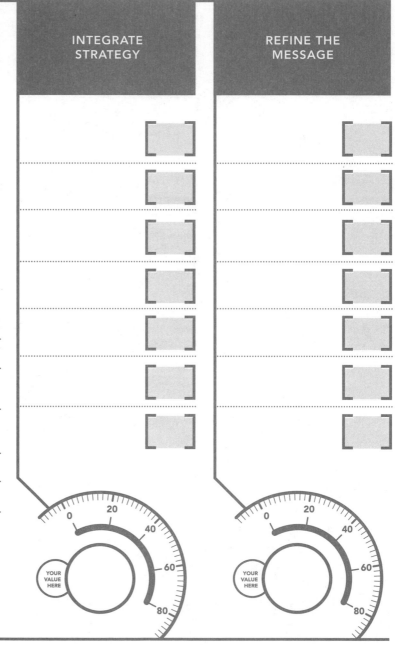

INTEGRATE STRATEGY

REFINE THE MESSAGE

YOUR VALUE HERE

YOUR VALUE HERE

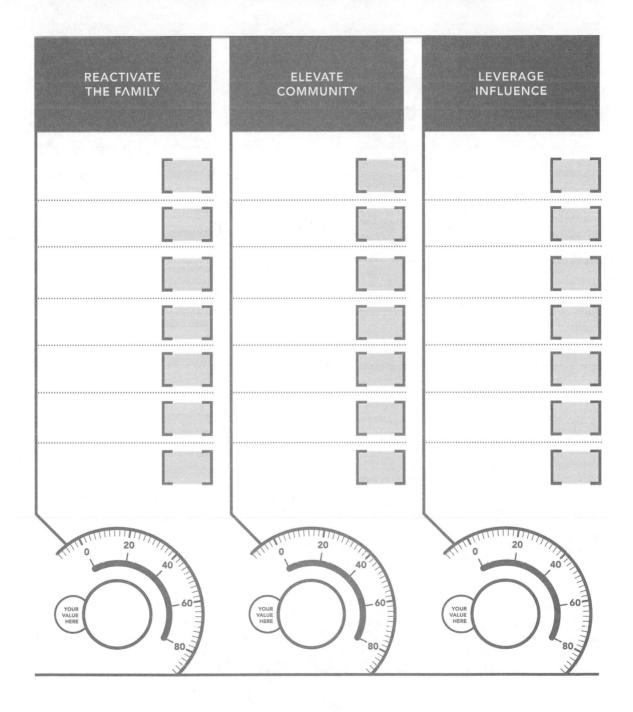

REACTIVATE THE FAMILY	ELEVATE COMMUNITY	LEVERAGE INFLUENCE

APPENDIX

PLANNING SHEET

Use this sheet to create a specific action plan for addressing each component that needs work in your ministry. Download more copies at OrangeLeaders.com.

COMPONENT _____
(Synchronized Team, Strategic Teaching, Compelling Vision, etc.)

1 Investigate: How are you really doing with this?

2 Idealize: Brainstorm new ideas about how to improve this or add it to your ministry.

3 Identify: Refine all your brainstormed ideas down to the best ones.

4 Implement: Establish an action plan to address these ideas, including specific steps, assignments, and deadlines.

AGENDA FOR FAMILY MINISTRY TEAM MEETING

STRATEGY

DATE:

PEOPLE INVOLVED:

LOCATION:

Who are you inviting to be part of your Family Ministry team who will add value in this particular area? When and where will you meet?

What things are you doing well?
How will you celebrate this?

What three quick fixes do you need to make?
When could you have these done, and who can help you?

What three long-term changes do you need to work toward?
What steps will you take to get there?

Who needs to be involved in these changes, and by what date should they be achieved? At what times will you check your progress and adjust?

In your ministry team meetings, focus on addressing some questions based on the Family Ministry Threads. You can start with the suggestion questions we listed, but feel free to create your own as well.

LEARNING THREAD
What books are we reading as a team?

What off site meetings have we planned as a team?

What responsibilities are we assigning team members outside of their regular tasks to help them expand their knowledge base?

What learning environments/conferences will we attend together?

TRANSITION THREAD
What kind of orientation do we have for parents, kids, and students transitioning into
… preschool?
… elementary?
… middle school?
… high school?
… college?

What printed/electronic materials have we established that help families understand how all the age group ministries work together?

How is the calendar synchronized to promote students at strategic times?

AGENDA FOR FAMILY MINISTRY TEAM MEETING

M

MESSAGE

DATE:

PEOPLE INVOLVED:

LOCATION:

Who are you inviting to be part of your Family Ministry team who will add value in this particular area? When and where will you meet?

What things are you doing well?
How will you celebrate this?

What three quick fixes do you need to make?
When could you have these done, and who can help you?

What three long-term changes do you need to work toward?
What steps will you take to get there?

Who needs to be involved in these changes, and by what date should they be achieved? At what times will you check your progress and adjust?

In your ministry team meetings, focus on addressing some questions based on the Family Ministry Threads. You can start with the suggestion questions we listed, but feel free to create your own as well.

PRODUCTION THREAD
What new tools are we using to capture the imagination?

What musical, drama, or technical talent can we share to help each other's ministries?

What about equipment? Are there new technologies we can share?

How are we rotating to evaluate each other's environments and give input?

CONTENT THREAD
What experiences can we create that enhance the content?

Who are some volunteers/leaders we can coach to be great communicators?

How can we make sure every leader and parent understands the master plan?

What kind of promotions and decorations are we using to enhance the weekly content or monthly themes?

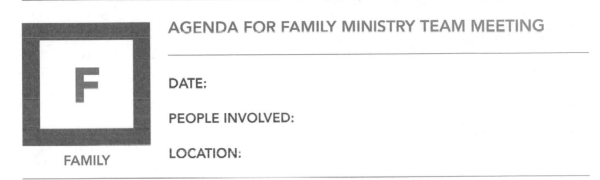

AGENDA FOR FAMILY MINISTRY TEAM MEETING

DATE:

PEOPLE INVOLVED:

LOCATION:

FAMILY

Who are you inviting to be part of your Family Ministry team who will add value in this particular area? When and where will you meet?

What things are you doing well?
How will you celebrate this?

What three quick fixes do you need to make?
When could you have these done, and who can help you?

What three long-term changes do you need to work toward?
What steps will you take to get there?

Who needs to be involved in these changes, and by what date should they be achieved? At what times will you check your progress and adjust?

In your ministry team meetings, focus on addressing some questions based on the Family Ministry Threads. You can start with the suggestion questions we listed, but feel free to create your own as well.

PARENT THREAD

How does a parent connect with the information they need from our church?

What consistent resources are going home, and are they being used?

Are there parent focus groups we can establish to give us input?

Who are the influential parents who can champion the partnerships to other parents?

What small group studies or materials can we use to cast vision to parents?

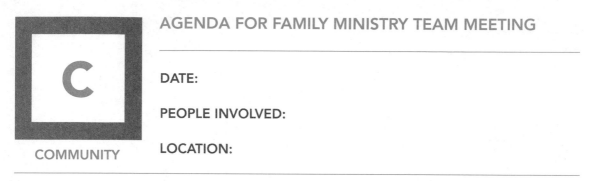

AGENDA FOR FAMILY MINISTRY TEAM MEETING

COMMUNITY

DATE:

PEOPLE INVOLVED:

LOCATION:

Who are you inviting to be part of your Family Ministry team who will add value in this particular area? When and where will you meet?

What things are you doing well?
How will you celebrate this?

What three quick fixes do you need to make?
When could you have these done, and who can help you?

What three long-term changes do you need to work toward?
What steps will you take to get there?

Who needs to be involved in these changes, and by what date should they be achieved? At what times will you check your progress and adjust?

In your ministry team meetings, focus on addressing some questions based on the Family Ministry Threads. You can start with the suggestion questions we listed, but feel free to create your own as well.

GROUP THREAD

What is the ratio of leaders to kids and students in our groups?

What are we doing to raise the value of community for every age group?

What events are we hosting to raise the level of participation?

Do we have clearly-defined, measurable goals for groups?

Are we getting unsolicited feedback from kids/teenagers who say they are enjoying their group experience?

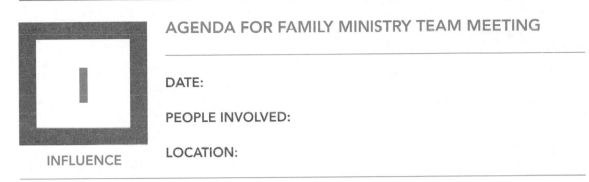

AGENDA FOR FAMILY MINISTRY TEAM MEETING

DATE:

PEOPLE INVOLVED:

LOCATION:

INFLUENCE

Who are you inviting to be part of your Family Ministry team who will add value in this particular area? When and where will you meet?

What things are you doing well?
How will you celebrate this?

What three quick fixes do you need to make?
When could you have these done, and who can help you?

What three long-term changes do you need to work toward?
What steps will you take to get there?

Who needs to be involved in these changes, and by what date should they be achieved? At what times will you check your progress and adjust?

What percentage of the students are plugging in to ministry?

What can we do to make sure all adult ministry team leaders are apprenticing students?

How are we getting families and teenagers involved in local and global efforts?

In your ministry team meetings, focus on addressing some questions based on the Family Ministry Threads. You can start with the suggestion questions we listed, but feel free to create your own as well.

VOLUNTEER THREAD
Are we creating regular and varied opportunities for teenagers to serve?

APPENDIX

NOTES

CHAPTER 2
THINK APPLES
[1] Robert A. Burgelman and George W. Cogan, "Intel Corp.: The DRAM Decision," *Harvard Business Review*, January 1989.

CHAPTER 4
INTEGRATE STRATEGY
[1] Andy Stanley, Reggie Joiner, and Lane Jones. *Seven Practices of Effective Ministry* (Sisters, OR: Multnomah, 2004).
[2] *First Knight*, directed by Jerry Zucker (Hollywood, CA: Columbia Pictures Industries, Inc.), 1995.

CHAPTER 5
REFINE THE MESSAGE
[1] Andy Stanley and Lane Jones. *Communicating for a Change: Seven Keys to Irresistible Communication* (Colorado Springs: Multnomah, 2006), p. 146.
[2] http://www.hanshofmann.net/quotes.html.
[3] Matthew 22:37–39.
[4] Rick Warren, foreword to Dan Kimball, *Emerging Church: Vintage Christianity for New Generations* (Grand Rapids, MI: Zondervan, 2003).
[5] Ephesians 4:15.
[6] John 1:14.
[7] *Braveheart*, directed by Mel Gibson (Hollywood, CA: Twentieth Century Fox), 1995.

CHAPTER 6
REACTIVATE THE FAMILY
[1] George Barna, "Parents Accept Responsibility for Their Child's Spiritual Development but Struggle with Effectiveness," *The Barna Update*, May 6, 2003.

[2] Winston Churchill, Richard Langworth, Lady Soames, Martin Gilbert. *Churchill By Himself: The Definitive Collection of Quotations* (Jackson, TN: PublicAffairs Perseus, 2008), 517.
[3] *The Incredibles*, directed by Brad Bird (Hollywood, CA: Walt Disney Pictures), 2004.

CHAPTER 7
ELEVATE COMMUNITY
[1] Mark Kelley, "LifeWay Research: Parents, Churches Can Help Teens Stay in Church," http://www.lifeway.com/lwc/article_main_page/0,170,A%253D165950%2526M%253D200812,00.html (accessed 13 July 2009).
[2] Ibid.
[3] Anne Lamott, *Traveling Mercies: Thoughts on Faith* (New York: Anchor Books, 2000), 100.
[4] *Finding Forrester*, directed by Gus Van Sant (Hollywood, CA: Columbia Pictures Corporation), 2000.

CHAPTER 8
LEVERAGE INFLUENCE
[1] Psalm 78:4–7
[2] *Pay it Forward*, directed by Mimi Leder (Hollywood, CA: Warner Brothers Pictures), 2000.

CHAPTER 9
ALIGNMENT
[1] Edward Catmull, "How Pixar Fosters Collective Creativity." *Harvard Business Review*, September, 2008.
[2] *Up*, directed by Pete Docter and Bob Peterson (Hollywood, CA: Walt Disney Pictures and Pixar Animation Studios), 2009.

REGGIE JOINER

ABOUT THE AUTHOR

Photo by
Ken Hawkins

Reggie Joiner is the founder and CEO of the reThink Group, a nonprofit organization providing resources and training to help churches maximize their influence on the spiritual growth of the next generation. The reThink Group provides innovative resources and training for leaders who work with preschoolers, children, families, and students. They have partners throughout the United States and eight other countries. The reThink Group is also the architect and primary sponsor of the Orange Conference and the Orange Tour, which provide national training opportunities for senior pastors, church leaders, and ministry volunteers.

Reggie is also one of the founding pastors, along with Andy Stanley, of North Point Community Church in Alpharetta, Georgia. In his role as executive director of Family Ministry, Reggie developed the concepts of ministry for preschool, children, students, and married adults over the course of his eleven years with the church. During his time with North Point Ministries, Reggie created KidStuf, a weekly environment where kids bring their parents to learn about God, as well as

Grow Up, an international conference to encourage and equip churches to create relevant, effective environments for children, families, and teenagers.

Reggie is the author of *Think Orange: Imagine the Impact When Church and Family Collide* and coauthor of *7 Practices of Effective Ministries* along with Lane Jones and Andy Stanley. He and his wife, Debbie, live in Cumming, Georgia, and have four grown children: Reggie Paul, Hannah, Sarah, and Rebekah.

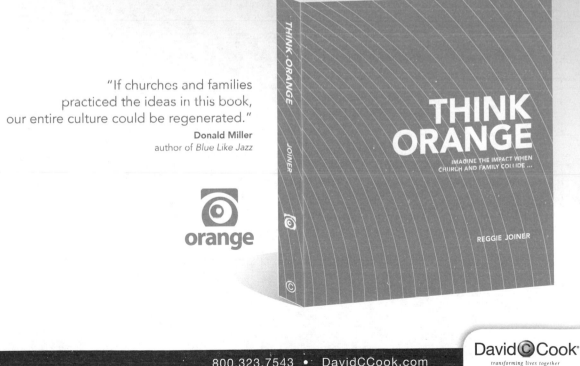

3 age-appropriate curriculums built around one strategy.
3 stages of life.
1 end in mind.

first look

FIRST LOOK www.myfirstlook.org

God made me.

God loves me.

Jesus wants to be my friend forever.

↓

252 BASICS

252 BASICS www.252basics.org

I need to make the wise choice.

I can trust God no matter what.

I should treat others the way I want to be treated.

↓

XP3

XP3 www.xp3students.org

I am created to pursue an authentic relationship with my Creator.

I belong to Jesus Christ and define who I am by what He says.

I exist every day to demonstrate God's love to a broken world.

RETHINK

A PREMIER GATHERING FOR LEADERS WHO ARE INFLUENCING THE NEXT GENERATION.

ORANGE IS THREE CONFERENCES IN ONE.

IT IS DESIGNED TO BRING YOUR SENIOR LEADERSHIP, COLLEGE, STUDENT, CHILDREN & PRESCHOOL MINISTRIES TOGETHER TO DISCUSS INNOVATIVE WAYS TO COLLECTIVELY IMPACT THE NEXT GENERATION.

If you value your influence in your community...

If you hope to engage the hearts of families...

If you desire to integrate with leaders...

If you want truth to make a permanent mark...

If you want relationships to become authentic...

THEN MAKE ORANGE CONFERENCE A PRIORITY.

WWW.THEORANGECONFERENCE.COM

Orange Leaders is an online curriculum that provides training materials for leaders and volunteers in every age-group ministry. Learn with other leaders through the blog, discussion board, or podcasts, all free. Additionally, subscribe to the Orange Leaders Curriculum to receive monthly training modules for ministry leaders and volunteers.

Learn more at www.OrangeLeaders.com